RS

TECHNICAL BOOKS
Chosen by Engineers for Engineers
Tel: 0536 201201

This book
Belongs to:
_____
_____
_____

9529

GAINING AND MAINTAINING THE NEW QUALITY STANDARD

GAINING AND MAINTAINING THE NEW QUALITY STANDARD

The BS EN ISO 9000 Tool Kit

Mike Mirams
and
Paul McElheron

FT
PITMAN
PUBLISHING

PITMAN PUBLISHING
128 Long Acre, London WC2E 9AN

A Division of Pearson Professional Limited

First published as *The Quality Tool Kit* 1994
This edition 1995

© Mike Mirams and Paul McElheron 1994, 1995

British Library Cataloguing in Publication Data
A CIP catalogue record for this book can be obtained from the British Library.

ISBN 0 273 61777 X

1 3 5 7 9 10 8 6 4 2

Phototypeset in Linotron Times Roman
by Northern Phototypesetting Co. Ltd, Bolton
Printed and bound in Great Britain
by Biddles Ltd, Guildford and King's Lynn

The Publishers' policy is to use paper manufactured from sustainable forests.

CONTENTS

SECTION D
Appendices

PREFACE TO THE SECOND EDITION

Those readers looking at quality systems to the standard of BS EN ISO 9000 for the first time can (and probably should) ignore this preface, which is intended for those who have knowledge or experience of the old BS 5750 and ISO 9000 Standards, prior to their revision in 1994.

The first edition of this book, entitled *The Quality Tool Kit*, was conceived and written during 1992 and 1993 and published in April 1994. During this period the various national and international committees that devise, write and amend the Standards for quality systems were meeting to consider various revisions to the existing Standards, namely the British Standard BS 5750, the European Standard EN 29000 and the International Standards Organisation's ISO 9000 (all of which were, more or less, equivalent). The revision was scheduled to be formally adopted in 1993 as part of an on-going programme of development, but delays in the bureaucratic process meant that it did not come into effect until the summer of 1994. Since that time all three Quality System Standards are now officially identical and abide under the title of BS EN ISO 9000, 1994.

The objects of the revisions included the correction of errors and inconsistencies that came to light during the use of the Standards. Indeed there were many unclear and incongruous elements and, to a large extent, these have been eliminated. It has also been attempted to make the Standards more acceptable and interpretable to organisations other than manufacturing industry. In the opinion of the authors this has only partly happened, but it is difficult to see how a set of requirements specifically developed for the manufacturing sector can ever be totally relevant and applicable to service industries and other non-manufacturing bodies. However, it will hopefully be seen from the text of *Gaining and Maintaining the New Quality Standard* that the Standards can be related to the needs of such organisations (and have been in the case of hundreds of successful accreditations by service orientated bodies), but the bias remains very strongly towards manufacturing.

SUMMARY OF CHANGES

Any reader wishing to examine in detail the changes due to the 1994 update is recommended to study the *Guide to the 1994 Revision of BS 5750/ISO 9000*, published by the BSI Quality Assurance, reference E313 Issue 1. Apart from the new title, BS EN ISO 9000, brief details of the most significant changes follow.

Numbering of clauses

The 20 main clauses of the old BS 5750/ISO 9000 Standards remain essentially the same although some have had their titles amended slightly. The prime change here is the fact that the main clause numbering is now the same for BS EN ISO 9001, 9002 and 9003. For example, Control of Non-conforming Product, formerly clause 4.13 in BS 5750 part 1/ISO 9001, 4.12 in part 2/9002 and 4.8 in part 3/9003, is now clause 4.13 universally. This means that in BS EN ISO 9002 and 9003 certain clauses will not apply (4.4, Design Control, for example).

In addition there have been a number of changes to sub-clauses, both in the splitting of the meatier ones into smaller morsels and in the addition of extra requirements. Care will thus be needed by those familiar with the old Standards in relating to the new clause numbering; a reference to clause 4.5.2 could be regarding either Document Changes or Document and Data Approval and Issue, depending on whether the pre- or post-revision version of ISO 9001 is being used. With ISO 9002 and 9003, the situation is even more complicated!

Attempts to make BS EN ISO 9000 more acceptable to non-manufacturing organisations

Previously, about the only attempt to relate a 'service' to a 'product' was an 'as appropriate' note in clause 3, Definitions. A product has now been a little better defined as including 'services, hardware and software', and being 'tangible or intangible (e.g. concepts or knowledge, etc.)'. Whether this will make BS EN ISO 9000, 1994 more readily understood and enthusiastically received by the non-manufacturing fraternity remains to be seen. One area of improvement for organisations not used to dealing with written contracts is the reduction in emphasis on the 'contract' in favour of references to customer 'requirements' and 'satisfaction'; this will appeal to many smaller operations, especially in the service sector.

Clarification of requirements

Prior to the revisions, in some cases it was unclear whether procedures should be documented or not. In some clauses it was a specific requirement, in others it was seemingly left to the interpretation of the user. All procedures are now expressly required to be documented, as opposed to merely being 'established and maintained'. Although it would have been difficult to become accredited to BS 5750/ISO 9000 without having documented procedures (since it has always been necessary to prove that operations were performed in accordance with the procedures), it is now made crystal clear from the outset that the quality system must be totally documented.

As stated above, many of the more substantial clauses have been split into smaller parts and there are several additional sub-clauses. This, along with changes to the text, has had the effect generally of clarifying many areas that were previously somewhat 'woolly' and open to interpretation. Other inconsistencies in the approach to quality systems have also been cleared up.

Upgrading of ISO 9002 and 9003

The element of servicing (of the after-sales variety) has been introduced to BS EN ISO 9002, making Design Control the only clause of BS EN ISO 9001 not present in 9002.

BS EN ISO 9003 now includes the Contract Review, Purchaser Supplied Product, Corrective (and Preventive) Action and Internal Quality Audits clauses. Although this raises its profile considerably, it is still described as a Standard for Inspection and Test only, and is considered still to be of limited use and value.

THE EFFECT OF THE REVISIONS ON ORGANISATIONS PREVIOUSLY REGISTERED TO BS 5750/ISO 9000, 1987

Organisations already accredited to the old versions of the Standards (or on their way to accreditation) need have nothing to fear from the introduction of the revised versions. Although the new Standards now apply to both potential and existing registered establishments, their implications are likely to have little significance to those with established quality systems, which, in all probability, are in accordance with the revised BS EN ISO 9000 anyway. Where this is not the case, and systems need modifying to bring them into line with the new requirements, the worst that can happen is that the situation will be treated as a minor non-conformity by the accrediting authority, and the organisation will have the opportunity to update its systems within an agreed period of time. No establishment is likely to lose its registration purely as a result of the changes in the requirements of the revised Standards, provided that the intention to conform is there and that action towards making the necessary minor amendments to its quality system in line with the new Standards is forthcoming.

IN CONCLUSION

We apologise if this preface concerning the changes to BS 5750/ISO 9000 seems a little cynical in places! The revisions, although not addressing some of the major weaknesses of the Standards (e.g. its application to non-manufacturing organisations, the bureaucracy and costs involved in its implementation and accreditation, etc.), are in most cases definite improvements; your authors are just a little concerned that the hundreds of man-hours in committee rooms in the four corners of the globe have come up with nothing more than what are essentially cosmetic changes! However, watch this space – a further revision is planned for 1998 with the intention of introducing elements in line with the world-wide movement towards total quality management.

We still remain convinced that BS EN ISO 9000 is a Quality Standard well worth attaining, both in terms of the benefits of accreditation and the internal benefits of implementing quality procedures to this level (see chapter 2). In this second edition, we have addressed all the clauses and sub-clauses of BS EN ISO 9000 in the revised format and their implications for organisations wishing to pursue accreditation. All the text has been updated, as have also the audit guides, checklists and sample documentation.

INTRODUCTION

The first edition of this book was called *The Quality Tool Kit*. A tool kit gives the impression of building something, and that is what the achievement of BS EN ISO 9000 is all about, building quality into our products and services by implementing systems that conform to international standards.

As with building anything from a plastic model aircraft to a full-size jumbo jet, from a garden shed to a stately home, we need plans, materials, labour and tools. We tackle the project piece by piece in a logical sequence, with continual reference to the plans. We may leave one part for a while, perhaps while the paint dries, but we will return later to complete it. Many craftsmen may be involved, all working as a team, and each with his or her own particular skills and objectives, but each with the common goal of completing the project. Eventually the garden shed or jumbo jet is completed, but that is not necessarily the end of the project. It will have to be maintained for it to last as long as is required and it is quite likely that some modifications to improve its performance would be advantageous in the future. Also, during the course of building we may have made mistakes from which we can learn, and will certainly have widened our experience. We can use this to develop the product, both the one we have just completed and any that we build in the future.

This second edition, *Gaining and Maintaining the New Quality Standard: The BS EN ISO 9000 Tool Kit*, is intended to be part of the tool kit, for those organisations aiming to build and maintain quality systems that meet the requirements of BS EN ISO 9000. Its intention is to give practical, down-to-earth assistance in simple language, and provide examples of quality system documentation, including a full quality manual. The main body of the work is a system of audit. This breaks down the complexities of BS EN ISO 9000 into simple 'bite-size' pieces. The objective is that anyone can use it to assess his or her own organisation relative to the requirements of BS EN ISO 9000. The results of the audit will reveal what work is needed to be done in which areas of the organisation, and from this schedules and action plans can be drawn up. All, or sections, of the audit can be repeated as often as necessary. This will give an indication of the progress that has been made and provide the opportunity to modify action plans if needed.

In our experience there are many misunderstandings about quality, quality systems, and BS EN ISO 9000. Prior to introducing the audit system and the sample documentation, the following chapters are written in the hope of dispelling some of these misconceptions.

Mike Mirams and Paul McElheron

MIKE MIRAMS ASSOCIATES

Mike Mirams Associates provides assistance in the development and implementation of quality systems and total quality management programmes to manufacturers and service providers. With experience in the UK, Europe and Asia, our philosophy is one of guidance – helping our clients develop their own systems in accordance with the needs of their customers, their own operational requirements and those of the Standards to which they aspire, through effective training and people-development.

Mike Mirams Associates
53 Windsor Road
Buxton
Derbyshire SK17 7NS
United Kingdom.

Telephone/fax UK (01298) 77494

A complete set of A4-size masters of the Audit Checklist pages in section B of this book is available from the authors. These can be used time and again to make photocopied working documents, giving more space for written comments, allowing repeated audits to be recorded and avoiding the need to write on the book pages.

To receive a set, send your name and address and a cheque for £15.00 to cover the cost of production, VAT and return postage (UK), to the above address. (Price correct at time of publication; call or fax for overseas rates.)

SECTION A

1

QUALITY SYSTEMS

DEFINING QUALITY

Perhaps we should begin by attempting to define quality.

We would all recognise that a new Rolls-Royce, costing £100,000, is a quality motor car, but why? Because of its price? Because it is luxurious? Because the rich and famous own them? If that is the case, Mr Ordinary's ten-year-old, rusty Ford Escort, which cost him £350 and reliably gets him to work at the factory every day, certainly could not be described as a quality item, but which is more suitable for his needs?

Fitness for its purpose is one factor. The Escort gets him to work on time. It is inexpensive to run and repair. He can get into it in his boiler suit without worrying about oil stains on the sumptuous leather upholstery. At work he can drive easily into one of the spaces in the small car park, and when he gets home he doesn't have to worry that if one of the kids in the street bounces a football off the bonnet, he will face a £500 repair bill. The Escort suits Mr Ordinary's purpose better than a Rolls-Royce.

Value for money is another consideration. Mr Ordinary's Escort cost £350 and will probably last a couple of years. A Rolls-Royce would have to take him to work for the next 571 years to be as cost effective! (We'll not embark on appreciation/depreciation discussions here, trying to assess the likely value of a Rolls-Royce in the middle of the third millennium.) So the Escort certainly represents better value for money for Mr Ordinary.

What does this tell us about the quality of Mr Ordinary's car? It is fit for its purpose, gives value for the money spent, and meets his needs exactly – which makes it a quality motor car. In contrast, it would *not* meet the needs of a British ambassador abroad, who needs to impress potential clients and government officials with comfort, luxury, the finest British craftsmanship and attention to detail, rather than the purely functional requirement of going from A to B at low cost.

Quality for our purposes is therefore relative to need. The best level of quality is that which meets our requirements exactly and which represents best value for money. As purchasers, if we buy something that exceeds our needs, we are probably not getting best value for money. As product or service providers, if we supply over and above the needs of our customers, we are probably wasting money in the supply process. Conversely, when purchasing, we might be able to buy something cheaper, but if it doesn't meet our needs it will not be of high enough quality. When supplying to our customers, even if our prices are low, if our products or services do not meet their needs, they will seek better quality elsewhere.

The key then, as manufacturers, suppliers or service providers, is to determine the needs of our customers and meet those needs at the price they are willing to pay; then and only then can we say we are providing the best quality. So, our definition of quality:

Quality is *fitness for purpose* and *value for money* but, above all, *meeting the needs of the customer*.

THE CUSTOMER

This brings us to an interesting point: who is the customer? Take the case of a young boy going to the bicycle shop to buy a new sprocket for his bike. Easy – the boy is the customer. But think about it for a while, it's a little more complex than at first sight. Suppose the boy goes with his father, who will actually pay for the new sprocket. Who is now the customer? And who is the customer of the wholesaler of the sprockets? Is it the boy, his father, or the owner of the shop? To take the issue one stage further, who is the customer of the sprocket manufacturer? We can now add the wholesaler to the line-up, together with mail-order warehouses, sports and leisure centres, and any other organisation that buys either the bike on which the sprocket is fitted or sprockets as spare parts.

The answer is of course that they are all customers, ultimately, of the sprocket manufacturer. The difficulty is, however, that each will have his own requirements when it comes to buying sprockets: the boy will want them to be available quickly, so that his bike will be back on the road as soon as possible; his father will want easily understood fitting instructions and, no doubt, a low price. For the shop owner attractive packaging may be a priority to help generate sales in the shop, while the wholesaler will want packaging that enables him to fit as many as possible on the shelf, and identification to enable the stock to be readily entered on the computer. Mail-order companies will need large discounts for bulk purchases, while durability may be the key requirement for sports centres.

Similar situations occur in service environments. Take the case of a refectory in a college of further education financed by the county council: who is the customer? Is it the student who eats the meal, who will want a satisfying meal at a low cost, or the student's employer, who will want the meal to be eaten in an environment conducive to the student's continuing day of study? What about the college administration, who are responsible for providing the service and who will want the meals served as quickly and cost effectively as possible. If the refectory is funded by the county council, it too will have its own requirements, as will the electorate who put the councillors in office.

Those with interests in total quality management will be aware of the internal customer/supplier relationships within an organisation, introducing so many more possibilities for determining and meeting the needs of customers, but this is probably beginning to go beyond the scope of this work. However, any organisation concerned with quality needs to be aware of who their customers are before they can address all of their specific needs and thereby provide quality products and services.

QUALITY SYSTEMS

Through marketing processes we identify our customers, their needs, and how much they are prepared to spend to satisfy those needs. All we have to do now is produce those products and services and our organisation can thrive. But how will we ensure that:

- we design our products and services in accordance with the customer's requirements?
- we manufacture or provide the service consistently in line with the requirements?
- we use in our products only materials and services that enable us to meet the requirements?
- our management and staff are aware of all the requirements and are adequately trained?
- our manufacturing or service processes are capable of meeting the requirements?
- quality controls will be adequate to maintain the standards?
- when things go wrong, they can be detected and corrected?

- we learn by our mistakes and develop in an environment of continuous improvement?

The answer to all these questions is: by the implementation of effective quality systems. Quality systems are means of ensuring that we design, produce and deliver our products and services to the specified quality, that is, to our customers' requirements.

Imagine a telesales clerk taking an order from a customer for a supply of widgets. He or she will write down the customer's name and the type and quantity of widgets required along with, possibly, other details. At the end of the day, the clerk will sign the sheets of paper containing all the orders taken during that day, and pass them to the warehouse.

The warehouse will make up and despatch all the orders in accordance with the details on the sheets, initialling each order on the sheet to indicate that the appropriate quantity of the required widget has been despatched to the specified client. If the warehouse cannot complete the order, say because of insufficient stock, the order sheet is marked accordingly, and the warehouse manager will note the shortage in the 'Incomplete Orders' book. This book is reviewed daily when supplies of new materials are received so that outstanding orders can be completed as soon as possible.

The order sheets are returned to the telesales department and checked by the clerk. Where any order cannot be completely fulfilled, the clerk telephones the customer to explain the situation and give an estimate of when delivery is likely to take place.

The above is an example of a basic quality system for a sales and despatch office. Its purpose is to ensure that:

- orders are processed;
- the correct items are supplied, in the correct quantities;
- orders that cannot be completed immediately are completed as soon as possible;
- customers are kept informed of any likely delays in deliveries;
- records are kept in case of queries or misunderstandings later.

The system should also identify and clarify who is responsible for which tasks.

This quality system may have been devised by someone in the sales or despatch office, or it may simply have evolved in the course of time and the light of experience. It may be a documented process, or be passed on from one staff member to another, or indeed different staff members may operate slightly different systems. The paperwork may involve specially produced forms, or comprise notes written on pieces of scrap paper. Whatever, it is a quality system, a system in place with the purpose of meeting the needs of the customer. How effective it is probably depends largely on which of these 'maybes' apply.

Probably all organisations have some quality systems in at least some areas of their operations. How effective they are in meeting the organisation's objectives for quality will depend on:

- how well thought out the systems are, particularly in relation to meeting the needs of the customers;
- the commitment of management and staff to making quality systems work;
- whether they are followed uniformly by all staff on all occasions;
- whether staff have been trained in their use;
- whether records are maintained to enable their effectiveness to be measured;
- whether the information that the systems provide is used to make improvements to the organisation's products and/or services.

Quality systems can range from the very simple and basic, such as a procedure to ensure that the telephone is answered quickly and politely, to the highly complex, like procedures for processes in a petrochemical plant. What they have in common is their objective: to help the organisation meet the needs of its customers.

THE BENEFITS OF AN EFFECTIVE QUALITY SYSTEM

There are many benefits to be derived from implementing quality systems in any organisation, including the following.

Increased customer satisfaction

Because the organisation's business is based more on meeting the customer's needs, better retention of customers will result; in fact, existing customers are likely to place increasing amounts of business with the organisation.

Reduced wastage

Effective quality systems enable an organisation to meet the needs of its customers and produce what is required, no more and no less. Also, procedures relating to the analysis and treatment of non-conforming product and the emphasis on preventive measures to deal with failures, cause scrap and rework to diminish.

Employee morale

The necessary involvement of staff, and the fact that they are positively contributing to the end product is a morale-booster. They know what to do and why they are doing it, and the question of who has responsibility for what is clarified.

More efficient and responsive organisation

Staff involvement leads to an organisation which is more motivated. As time goes on employees become used to their new ways of working and putting quality first. The 'right first time' philosophy becomes instinctive.

Better position in the market place

Being more efficient and cost effective leads naturally to the organisation having the edge over its competitors.

Bigger profits

This is the end result of all of the above!

CASE HISTORY

We close the chapter with a true case history where the implementation of quality systems solved some real problems, and made the organisation demonstrably much more profitable. Details and names have been omitted.

A substantial manufacturing company (X) supplies sub-assemblies to a well-known manufacturer (Y) of high-quality consumer products. X and Y have an agreed system of recharges: for every defective item supplied,

Y is entitled to levy a charge on X, based on the amount of labour and materials required to put the defects right on Y's premises. These charges were running at tens of thousands of pounds per annum for X, and Y was being frustrated by the resultant delays that caused problems with supplies to its own customers.

After much pressure from Y, and having looked very closely at its own operation, X decided to try to implement some fairly basic quality systems in its factory, with the objective of drastically reducing the defects found by Y. With consultancy help, X set up systems to inspect and test raw materials and control its suppliers, make in-process controls to detect faults as early as possible in the production lines, and take greater care in finished product inspections. Greater emphasis was placed on checking and comparing with the customer's samples and specifications, and reference to quality reports specially requested from the customer. Within two months, the rate of rejects from Y had fallen by over 85 per cent, with a consequent huge reduction in recharges.

The improvements were sustained, and Y was delighted and awarded X its 'Supplier of the Year' award. However, the story doesn't end there. Back at X's factory, although the quality of product leaving the works had improved so dramatically, there was now a problem of rejects occurring in the production processes, picked up by in-process inspections. Further systems were implemented, along with additional training for line operatives, to empower all of them to inspect their own material (whether components or sub-assemblies) and accept it for processing in their own operations only if perfect – they had work instructions and examples to measure against. Non-conforming product was isolated from the lines and the operatives, supervisors and line managers met daily to review it, determine the causes of failures, and devise ways of ensuring that these problems would not recur. In this way, the 15 per cent production reject rate was systematically reduced to just over 1 per cent in the course of about six months.

The results of these exercises are that Y has placed an increasing amount of business with X, being highly satisfied with the increased level of reliability in its supplies. In addition, the savings to X in terms of reduced recharges from Y and fewer rejects in manufacturing amounted to an estimated £85,000 per annum. The one-off cost of implementing the systems, including consultants' fees and all expenses, was less than £8,000.

SUMMARY

- Quality is fitness for purpose, value for money, and meeting the needs of the customer.
- In order to meet the needs of customers, we need to know who they are (all of them) and what are their requirements.
- Quality systems are the means of providing products and services to meet the needs of customers.
- There are many benefits to be derived from implementing effective quality systems, to both the customer and the supplier.

In the next chapter we shall look at the national and international standards for quality systems, BS EN ISO 9000.

2

BS EN ISO 9000

HISTORY

In order to understand what BS EN ISO 9000 is, why it is so important in the business world today, and why it exists in the form it does, it is necessary first to investigate its history.

In the 1950s and early 1960s the Ministry of Defence was experiencing a number of problems with breakdowns of equipment provided by manufacturers and suppliers. With the defence of the nation at stake, along with the health and safety of forces personnel, it was clearly vital for the equipment to be as reliable as possible. The Ministry therefore introduced what were known as Defence Standards, quality procedures that had to be documented and implemented by designers, manufacturers and suppliers of military equipment. Their main purpose was to assure the Ministry that products conformed with its specifications.

In the 1970s the Defence Standards were incorporated into the AQAP Standards, which are those still used today by North Atlantic Treaty Organisation (NATO) countries for the supply of defence equipment.

Meanwhile, as the benefits of the AQAP Standards in Ministry of Defence establishments and suppliers were being noticed in the outside world, the need for quality systems, and a standard by which they could be measured, was being felt in other manufacturing industries. This led in 1979 to the launch of BS 5750 as the recognised measure of quality systems for industries not associated with the supply of defence equipment. BS 5750 was based very much on the AQAP Standards; the main difference for suppliers wishing to have their quality systems accredited is that the Ministry of Defence itself assesses its suppliers to AQAP standard, while organisations seeking accreditation to BS 5750 had their systems assessed by an independent approval body at their own expense (see chapter 3).

Due to international demand, in 1987 the international standard for quality systems, ISO 9000, was established. This was the direct equivalent of the then latest version of BS 5750 (1987), and gained rapidly in its acceptance as a recognised world standard for quality systems. During the early 1990s ISO 9000 went through a process of revision, the intention of which was to correct inconsistencies and errors that had come to light in the course of world-wide usage, and to improve the wording of the Standard and make it more applicable to organisations other than those engaged in manufacturing industry. The revised Standard was formally adopted in 1994 by the International Standards Organisation and by BSI, and is renamed (as far as the UK is concerned) BS EN ISO 9000.

Such is the acceptability of the modern Standards that it is quite likely that NATO will end its dependence on AQAP Standards (along with its associated costs to defence ministries) in favour of BS EN ISO 9000.

RELEVANCE

Today, the implementation of quality systems is no longer confined to defence and manufacturing industry. It will be appreciated from the brief history given above that BS EN ISO 9000, having been conceived and brought up in a defence/manufacturing environment, may not at first sight appear to be 100 per cent relevant to today's more diverse business world. As we delve more deeply into the Standards later in this book, however, it will be seen that for the most part they are indeed relevant. What is frequently confusing is the style in which they are written, along with the jargon and terminology used. Various attempts have been made to address specific quality issues in specific sectors by the assessing bodies and others, including BS 5750 part 8, 'Guide to quality management and quality systems elements for services'. However, the Standards themselves rule.

BS EN ISO 9000 is to a degree self-perpetuating. One of its requirements is that an accredited organisation (i.e. one that has had its quality system approved to BS EN ISO 9000) will take into account the quality systems of its existing and potential suppliers when assessing those suppliers' suitability to provide materials and/or services. It is thus becoming desirable (if not essential in some cases) for such suppliers to be able to demonstrate their commitment to quality by being themselves accredited, or at least in the process of so becoming. This in turn has a knock-on effect on the suppliers' suppliers, and so on. The result is that many organisations without the appropriate accreditation are finding their markets diminishing as potential customers turn their backs on them.

As a reaction to this some organisations are refusing to take any interest in becoming accredited, regarding the whole process as bureaucracy gone mad, even though it would benefit them to do so. It is often a case of not seeing the wood for the trees; people can easily be blinded by the cost and effort involved, without appreciating the real benefits that effective quality systems can bring, and the increased markets that BS EN ISO 9000 accreditation makes available. Unfortunately BS EN ISO 9000 has acquired a reputation (not always undeserved) of being excessively complicated, time-consuming and costly to implement. Consultancies make the most of the lack of understanding of the complexities of the Standards and are able to charge large fees for their services in steering organisations through the accreditation process, when, given appropriate guidance and training, the correct motivation and commitment, and some time, most can achieve it on their own with minimal outside help.

THE SCOPE OF BS EN ISO 9000

At this stage it is appropriate to give more details of the scope of the Standard. There are three parts to BS EN ISO 9000 (or the ISO 9000 series, as it is often referred to).

BS EN ISO 9001 is the Standard for quality systems relating to design, development, production, inspection and testing, installation and servicing. In other words, this Standard is appropriate to an organisation that provides products of its own (or subcontracted) designs, produces them, and delivers to the customer. If the organisation carries out installation and after-sales servicing, these too are covered.

BS EN ISO 9002 is as 9001 but covers production, inspection and testing, installation and servicing only; design is not included.

BS EN ISO 9003 is intended as a part of the Standard to apply to organisations involved in inspection and testing only, containing all the clauses of 9001 with the exception of design, purchasing, process control and after-sales servicing. As a result of the exclusions, the requirements of many of the other clauses are less stringent. BS EN ISO 9003 is generally of insufficient adequacy as a quality system for most organisations and therefore rarely used; when it is, its value is limited.

The operative part of BS EN ISO 9000 (clause 4) contains 20 sub-clauses or sections, all of which are applicable in BS EN ISO 9001; 19 are applicable in 9002 and 16 in 9003. The 20 clauses, and their relevance to each part, are shown in table 2.1. The full requirements of each clause or section are dealt with in detail in section B of this book, but a brief summary follows.

BS EN ISO 9001 is used as it contains all 20 clauses. It may help the reader to have a copy of BS EN ISO 9001 to hand, and/or a copy of BS 5750 part 4 (1995). The latter is a guide to BS EN ISO 9000. All

Table 2.1   The clauses of BS EN ISO 9000

Clause Number		BS EN ISO Standard Number		
		9001	9002	9003
4.1	Management responsibility	✔	✔	✗
4.2	Quality system	✔	✔	✗
4.3	Contract review	✔	✔	✔
4.4	Design control	✔	n/a	n/a
4.5	Document control	✔	✔	✔
4.6	Purchasing	✔	✔	n/a
4.7	Control of customer supplied product	✔	✔	✔
4.8	Product identification and traceability	✔	✔	✗
4.9	Process control	✔	✔	n/a
4.10	Inspection and testing	✔	✔	✗
4.11	Control of inspection, measuring and test equipment	✔	✔	✔
4.12	Inspection and test status	✔	✔	✔
4.13	Control of non-conforming product	✔	✔	✗
4.14	Corrective and preventive action	✔	✔	✗
4.15	Handling, storage, packaging, preservation and delivery	✔	✔	✔
4.16	Control of quality records	✔	✔	✗
4.17	Internal quality audits	✔	✔	✗
4.18	Training	✔	✔	✗
4.19	Servicing	✔	✔	n/a
4.20	Statistical techniques	✔	✔	✔

Those clauses of BE EN ISO 9003 identified with ✗ have a less stringent requirement compared with that for BS EN ISO 9001 and 9002.

these documents are published by the British Standards Institution; see appendices, in section D.

4.1 *Management responsibility* Describes the responsibilities of the organisation's management towards its objectives and policy for, and commitment to, quality.

4.2 *Quality system* The requirements for a documented quality system, including development and maintenance.

4.3 *Contract review* Describes the need for the organisation to make sure that all contracts are within its scope, and meet the requirements of the customer and the organisation.

4.4 *Design control* The ability to ensure that products and services are designed to meet the needs of the customer and the organisation.

4.5 *Document control* Describes the requirements to control and maintain all documentation related to the quality system.

4.6 *Purchasing* The need for the organisation to ensure that all materials and services bought in are of the necessary standard.

4.7 *Control of customer supplied product* Describes the requirements for controls as for purchased product.

4.8 *Product identification and traceability* The need to be able to identify materials, products and services in all stages of processing, and, if necessary, the ability to trace product by batch.

4.9 *Process control* The need to be able to apply controls to manufacturing processes and the provision of services to ensure that the requirements are met.

4.10 *Inspection and testing* Describes the requirements to apply inspections and tests to raw materials, processes (including services) and finished products and services to ensure conformance with requirements.

4.11 *Control of inspection, measuring and test equipment* The need to be able to verify that such equipment gives accurate results.

4.12 *Inspection and test status* All products and services must be identifiable as to whether or not they have passed the appropriate inspections and tests.

4.13 *Control of non-conforming product* Describes the need for material, products and services that do not meet the required standards to be isolated and dealt with appropriately.

4.14   *Corrective and preventive action*   Putting right things that go wrong and taking measures to ensure that they do not go wrong in the future.

4.15   *Handling, storage, packaging, preservation and delivery*   Describes the requirements to maintain the quality of the product until it reaches the customer; ensuring services reach the customer to the required standards.

4.16   *Control of quality records*   The requirements to establish and maintain records on all aspects related to quality.

4.17   *Internal quality audits*   Audits within the organisation are to be planned, carried out and documented to ensure that the quality system is working effectively.

4.18   *Training*   The need to determine training needs in the organisation and ensure that training is carried out effectively.

4.19   *Servicing*   The need to ensure that after-sales servicing meets the specified requirements.

4.20   *Statistical techniques*   When used, statistical techniques must be suitable for the processes, products and services.

THE SCOPE OF THE STANDARD v. THE SCOPE OF THE ORGANISATION

At this stage there may well be some difficulty in deciding which part of BS EN ISO 9000 is the most appropriate for an organisation. The following paragraphs should make things a little clearer.

Whole organisation or part?

It is not necessary to include all the activities of an organisation in the scope of its registration. For example, a cleaning company may in the first instance wish to seek accreditation for its industrial department only, and consider extending it to the commercial and domestic departments at a later stage. This would certainly limit the range of customers, activities and personnel that the quality system would have to relate to, and development of the system would therefore require less work. It would still however give the benefit of the increased markets in the industrial sector that its limited accreditation would provide.

Which part?

BS EN ISO 9001 would at first sight be appropriate for a company that designs and manufactures computers, and also has a department for after-sales service. However, in order to take things a step at a time, it could well initially seek accreditation to BS EN ISO 9002, in which case its design operations would not be included but all the manufacturing, supply and servicing aspects could be accredited. The company may or may not decide later to seek to extend its accreditation to 9001. This can often be a good way of spreading the cost and effort over a longer period while still gaining a 'prize' part way through the project.

Clauses that are not applicable

To many organisations, some sections of the Standard may be irrelevant. An accountancy practice may be interested in BS EN ISO 9001, as it would particularly like its creativity in designing special services for clients to be included. But the firm is certainly not involved in purchasing raw materials, after-sales servicing or statistical techniques! This would not prohibit the firm from going for 9001, but clauses 4.6, 4.19 and 4.20 would not apply because these functions do not exist.

Beware, however: if the functions *do* exist, they will have to come within the scope of the Standard. It is not possible to exclude a clause in the Standard in the same way as an area of activity in the organisation – the difference is important!

Service providers

As discussed previously, the Standards were developed from the needs of the Ministry of Defence and manufacturing industry, and therefore are seemingly biased away from the service provider. Reference is continually made to 'products', 'production', 'processes', etc. A little creative thought is needed to interpret and relate the requirements to the service-based organisation. Consider the following.

Design

It is easy to picture the design of a manufactured product – drawing boards, computer-assisted design, people in white coats, etc. But a service needs designing too: what it is to provide/not provide, how/when/how often/by whom it is to be provided, etc.

Production and processes

Rather than welding and screwing things together, production for the service organisation is the process of actually providing the service – designing the factory extension, repairing the photocopier or whatever.

Inspection and testing

Manufactured products can be subjected to physical inspections and tests to establish how well they have been produced. This is usually more difficult with a service, which cannot be weighed or measured, as such. However, there is still the need for them to be controlled, usually by inspection and testing of the results (e.g. testing a cleaned surface for bacteria, checking the temperature of an oven that has been repaired, and so on – much scope for the imagination here).

Handling, storage, packaging and delivery

Whereas handling, storage and packaging are difficult to relate to service organisations, except in so far as a product may be involved (a cooked meal, for example), delivery can be considered as the process of getting the service to the customer. This may simply mean that a repair job is performed just as effectively on the customer's premises as it is in the supplier's workshop.

After-sales service

With a service-based organisation this is largely irrelevant, as the product *is* the service. This can therefore generally be ignored.

THE BENEFITS AND COSTS OF ACCREDITATION TO BS EN ISO 9000

The benefits to an organisation of having effective quality systems were discussed in chapter 1. Having your quality system approved to BS EN ISO 9000 brings added benefits, among them:

- proving to your customers that you take quality seriously;
- the edge over your competitors who are not accredited;
- keys to open new doors, e.g. the opportunity to tender for contracts open only to accredited suppliers;
- the internal auditing procedures are a valuable tool in optimising and maintaining quality;
- increased protection against product liability (the approval of an organisation's quality systems is proof of its commitment to produce goods and services free of defects, and can support a supplier's case in the event of their safety or suitability being called into question);
- worldwide recognition of your commitment to quality.

However, there is no gain without pain. As with most things that bring something good, there is a price to pay. Before embarking on a course of action to implement quality systems and go for the prize of being accredited to BS EN ISO 9000, anyone would be well advised to consider the costs carefully, as they can sometimes be prohibitive, especially the non-financial ones.

There are four categories of cost to an organisation seeking accreditation: financial, commitment, culture and time. Some of the costs are one-offs, associated with the creation and implementation of the quality systems, and the application for and accreditation to the appropriate Standard. There are also ongoing costs after the organisation has gained the certificate; the quality systems must be maintained and developed, and the accrediting body will make occasional audits to check that the systems are still working, at a cost to the organisation. Although it is impossible within the scope of a work of this nature to estimate the actual level of costs, the following will give an indication of the areas in which costs are likely to arise.

Financial costs

Application and assessment fees are payable to the accrediting body to cover the process of registering the organisation's application and auditing its quality systems to assess compliance with the Standards. Then, annual registration and surveillance fees are again payable to the accrediting body for periodic audits and assessments, and continued accreditation.

Consultants' fees and expenses: clearly, the more work the organisation is able to put into the project using its own people, the less it will be dependent on outside experts. Frequently, however, some specialist input is desirable and/or necessary. In some cases grants are available to bear part of the cost of consultants' fees for the purpose of seeking BS EN ISO 9000 accreditation.

Additional staff: the amount of work necessary to complete a project such as this satisfactorily will depend on many factors, particularly the size and scope of the organisation and the standards of existing systems in relation to the requirements of BS EN ISO 9000. Depending on the availability of existing staff, it may be necessary to engage additional personnel.

Lost production: after implementation, effective quality systems will assist full production and make it more efficient. However, during the period of the 'learning curve', while systems are being devised and implemented on the shop floor, there is always the possibility that output will suffer, and organisations should be aware of this.

Equipment and materials: the quality system will require manuals, procedures, work instructions and forms to be developed. In the process of production, as drafts are considered and amended, a small rain-forest of paper will be required, together with binders, filing cabinets, etc. Also, additional word processing equipment may be necessary to avoid excessive drain on existing resources.

Commitment costs

It may seem strange to include commitment as a cost factor. However, commitment to a project such as this often means that commitment is removed (either fully or partly) from something else; from a factory extension or new product development, for example.

Commitment must come, and be seen to come, from the top (the chairman and chief executive) and flow through management to all strata of personnel. It is the commitment of money and other resources, time, effort and training. It is the commitment that remains as strong even after delays and possible disappointments, and must be continuous after accreditation has been achieved.

Culture costs

Why change? We've always got by this way in the past!

The change in culture, necessary in many organisations when becoming more quality orientated, is often the greatest difficulty to be overcome. It is vital to develop at all levels an awareness of quality and the desire to become more customer driven. Attitudes may need to be changed towards a philosophy of 'Get it right first time' and working in a structured manner, not to mention changes in procedures and paperwork.

In many cases, it may mean turning the organisation upside down and inside out, throwing out all the old ways of working and adopting completely new ones. The cost may be that the entire identity and culture of the organisation will be changed for ever, and consideration should be given in advance as to whether or not this a good thing

Time costs

Time is our most precious resource; we have very limited supplies of it, and once used it can never be recycled.

Implementing quality systems to BS EN ISO 9000 will take a lot of time. Even with small organisations with relatively simple systems, it will take a minimum of several months of consistent attention to achieve accreditation (it is necessary to be able to demonstrate a history of the systems working). With larger organisations it could take several years, depending on their size, scope of operations and the resources devoted to the project. What is guaranteed is that all staff will be involved in one way or another, and some will have to spend a large proportion of their time (perhaps *all* their time) on it.

Only the organisation concerned can determine the costs it is likely to incur during the course of developing its quality systems to achieve accreditation to BS EN ISO 9000; some additional guidance to the estimation process is given in chapter 3. It is vital, however, that the costs are carefully weighed against the benefits before embarking on the project, as the highest costs related to benefit received will be for the organisation that commences the journey but is unable to complete it for any reason. Consider also the organisation, and its position in the market place due to publicity, that gains BS EN ISO 9000 recognition only to lose it later because of its inability to maintain its systems.

SUMMARY

- The modern-day BS EN ISO 9000 Standard is based on the needs for quality equipment in defence.
- The Standard is becoming increasingly demanded and is relevant to all kinds of organisations, including service providers, although they are frequently difficult to relate to some operations.
- There is sufficient flexibility within the scope of the Standard and within most organisations to enable it to be applicable in most cases.
- There are benefits and costs to be weighed against each other before embarking on a project to implement quality systems to BS EN ISO 9000.

Having balanced the benefits against the costs, in the next chapter we look at some basic requirements in an organisation considering seeking accreditation.

3

ESSENTIAL FOUNDATIONS FOR QUALITY SYSTEMS TO BS EN ISO 9000

MOTIVATION

Depending on the benefits an organisation considers that it can derive from accreditation to BS EN ISO 9000, there are many motives for becoming involved in the process. As with most objectives, the correct motivation is often fundamental to success; therefore any organisation considering the implementation of quality systems and seeking approval to BS EN ISO 9000 would do well to consider its motives carefully before embarking on the course. Figure 3.1 presents the results of a survey of reasons for seeking BS 5750/ISO 9000 accreditation. (Information gathered by the authors during 1992/3, before the current title was adopted, from about 200 organisations expressing an interest in, or having gained, accreditation.)

Typical reasons for seeking accreditation include the following:

- to save money;
- to increase market share;
- to improve sales;
- prestige;
- our major competitors are accredited;
- our customers request/demand it;
- we wish to expand into overseas markets;
- to increase marketability;
- everyone in this sector is going for it;
- the chairman wants us to have it;
- to indicate that we are a professional organisation;

- the TEC is offering assistance;
- it's in our five-year plan.

Those motives which are customer-driven are the ones most likely to support the organisation through to accreditation. A customer-orientated organisation is, by definition, most likely to be quality conscious, and therefore most likely to succeed. Similarly, market-centred motives are an excellent basis for embarking on the project, provided the market research has been done correctly. Just because your competitors are accredited is not sufficient motivation unless there is (or is likely to be in the future) a genuine need in your market place. BS EN ISO 9000 accreditation that is built into strategic planning, rather than being an executive whim, has also a better chance of success.

Beware of prestige motives. BS EN ISO 9000 accreditation will certainly indicate to the world that you are a professional organisation, but do not try to put the cart before the horse – an organisation needs to be professional to gain accreditation, not the other way round. If your chairman wants the organisation to be accredited, his or her motivation

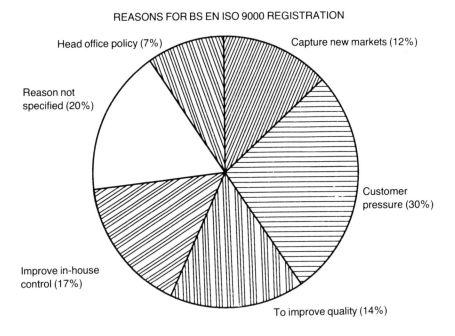

Fig. 3.1   1992/3 survey results

must first be analysed, found valid, and communicated to the management and all staff members; it then will become the motivation of the
organisation.

Some organisations, notably the Training and Enterprise Councils
(TECs), offer assistance to organisations seeking accreditation. This is
frequently by way of joint workshops with other bodies and possibly
subsidised consultancy. This can be an excellent help, particularly for
smaller organisations with limited resources, but bear in mind that the
TEC's motivation may be, partly at least, to meet its sponsor-set targets
for interesting organisations in becoming accredited and joining its
schemes. Being able to do it at subsidised cost is no justification on its
own.

For those whose motivation is reducing cost, quality systems can
undoubtedly save money in the long term by improved efficiency and the
reduction in waste. However, in the short term, the cost associated with
implementing systems can frequently outweigh the benefits. The real-life
example in the previous chapter, showing how X company saved so much
with so little expenditure in so short a time, will not apply in every case.
The amount and speed of cost-saving improvements will depend largely
on the existing efficiencies; generally, the greater the inefficiency the
greater the potential for savings, but the higher the likely cost of implementing appropriate systems.

Whatever the reasons for taking the decision to seek accreditation to
BS EN ISO 9000, it is important that the outcome is not just an attitude of
conformism as a result of slavishly documenting procedures to produce a
quality system. The end result should be a set of systems and procedures
which ensure that products and services meet customers' requirements
fully; a good system is one that involves all employees and capitalises on
their quality awareness. A word of warning: there have been many
instances of organisations abandoning quality improvement programmes
in order to concentrate on the documentation of their procedures in the
run-up to BS EN ISO 9000 assessment. This is obviously not a good thing
as the only result of several months of effort will be a piece of paper!

COMMITMENT

Motivation leads to commitment, also a vital ingredient for a long-term
project of this nature. In the previous chapter commitment was discussed
as being one of the categories of cost to an organisation of implementing

quality systems to BS EN ISO 9000, in that it may well be necessary to divert commitment from another area of the organisation in order to gain accreditation.

The need for commitment cannot be overemphasised; lack of it is probably the most common reason for failure. It must emanate from the top of the organisation and must be seen to be there, cascading through to all levels. All, from the most senior management to the lowest-ranking of personnel, full-time and part-time, permanent and temporary, must take not only an interest in quality but also responsibility for it.

Senior management must be proactive in all activities leading towards BS EN ISO 9000 accreditation. Key areas are:

- defining a clear and understandable quality policy;
- developing strategies;
- laying down areas of responsibility;
- constant monitoring of progress, and communicating that progress to all;
- giving understandable and precise instructions.

They must provide the necessary resources (finance, personnel, time and others) to enable the organisation to see the project through to gaining the BS EN ISO 9000 certificate, and beyond, to enable it to develop and continue to grow as a quality organisation. Success will be in question if, having allocated resources to the project, they are removed or reduced later when the going gets tough.

Management's attitudes may have to change to reflect the new quality culture, and those attitudes – and understanding – must transfer without loss to the employees. This, in itself, may require a degree of change in the way in which an organisation works. Employees must be permitted to become involved, and have the power to take actions and responsibility as far as quality is concerned. (Remember the case study in the previous chapter: the production operatives were given the authority to reject unsuitable material, and became involved in the process of determining the causes of problems and seeking ways of eliminating them.) Given the responsibility and the opportunity, staff at the 'sharp end' of processes are most likely to know best how to reduce defects and make improvements; the key is in motivating them and delegating the necessary authority. This will need the commitment of both management and the employees concerned, and will come about only through sound management practice, appropriate training, strong lines of communication, and recognition of successes.

THE ROLE OF MANAGEMENT AND STAFF

This leads us nicely to the point where we discuss in more detail the new roles that must be played in the quality-orientated organisation on its road to BS EN ISO 9000 accreditation.

All staff

Firstly, all staff must become customer-orientated. The fact that the sales and marketing departments are aware of the needs of the customer is insufficient to enable the organisation to produce a product or service that conforms to his or her requirements. The design department must be able to relate its work to the needs of the customer, *not* to what it thinks the customer needs. Production must provide the appropriate goods or services, and packing must ensure that they are packaged according to those needs; if this means making a new box to take 13 widgets instead of the usual 12, then so be it. If the customer wants delivery on Wednesday rather than Thursday (when the van is in the area), we must deliver (happily) on Wednesday. Once firmly established, the customer's requirements need to be transmitted to all areas of the organisation in order for them to be met.

We have probably all experienced a situation such as the following. The washing machine breaks down on Tuesday, and you call the repair company. 'We'll try to come on Thursday' is the promise. 'About what time will that be?' is your response, 'because I will have to take time off work to let the engineer in.' 'I can't tell you that, but would you prefer an a.m. or p.m. visit?' is the reply. You, realising that you are dealing with a bureaucratic empire builder, don't argue, but say that you would prefer as early as possible in the morning. Thursday morning comes – and goes. So does Thursday afternoon and the engineer has still not arrived. You have lost a day's work, and the only consolation offered by the repair company when you call them is: 'We never quote firm times – our engineer was delayed on another job. We'll try to call tomorrow; would you prefer an a.m. or p.m. visit?'

Although you emphasised that you would like an approximate arrival time for the engineer to enable you to minimise the amount of time you spent away from work, the repair company was clearly unable or unwilling to take account of your requirements as the customer, but preferred instead to go about its business in the way that best suited its own convenience. To become more quality orientated, and thus more geared to providing a service to the requirements of the customer, a company such as this must:

- redesign its service to relate to customer need;
- be prepared to make firm commitments to its customers;
- make all staff aware of those needs and commitments
- be able to fulfil those commitments through the company personnel.

Naturally, the provision of a service to meet the needs of the customer may involve additional cost (more engineers employed, for example), but the customer may well be willing to pay more if it enables him or her to take less time off work. Obviously, the company needs to talk to – and, more importantly, listen to – its customers.

This brings us to the second point; all staff must become involved in quality measures. In the example given above, who will bear the brunt of the customer's anger when the engineer finally arrives to repair the washing machine? Who is best placed to turn the customer's negative experience into something positive to assist the development of the organisation as a customer-driven, quality service provider? As we said before, it is the people at the 'sharp end' (in this case, either the person at the end of the telephone or the engineer) who are probably in the best position to determine the way products and services should be improved, and therefore have a major part to play in the development of quality policies and procedures; they must be encouraged to make their contribution by the appropriate motivation and reward.

Management

Senior management are the source of the commitment, but management in general have the responsibility of being the driving force behind a programme of this nature. Inspiration and initiatives may come (and should be encouraged to come) from anywhere in the organisation, but without management to make things happen, no progress will result. It must also be a team effort; no one person can see the project through on his or her own. Even though one person or department may be given the ultimate responsibility for facilitating the implementation of BS EN ISO 9000 systems, the project must have the support of all departments and departmental managers, because each will be involved.

The management representative

When we look in detail at the requirements of BS EN ISO 9000 it will become clear that it is necessary to have in the organisation one management representative with the responsibility and authority to ensure that the requirements of the Standards are implemented and maintained. This person is usually the quality manager (or the quality systems manager), and the success or otherwise of the project will depend largely on his or her attributes and abilities.

The management representative's prime role is not necessarily to devise and write manuals and procedures; which is best done by those who will be using them. The management representative is there to:

- ensure that the requirements of BS EN ISO 9000 are adhered to within the organisation;
- facilitate the implementation of systems;
- co-ordinate all activities towards the quality objectives;
- be a reference point in the organisation for staff, customers and outside parties (accrediting bodies, for example).

No matter how small the organisation, it needs someone in this role. He or she must have the authority to decide or delegate all matters relating to the quality systems; for example, it may be necessary to halt production, or divert resources from one department to another, while a quality issue is sorted out. The position must therefore be functionally close to senior management.

The management representative's position may not necessarily be full time; what *is* essential is that his or her other responsibilities do not create any possible conflict of interests. For example, it probably would not be a good idea for the production manager in a factory to be the management representative. The production manager will have targets set for production in both quantity and quality. If production quantities are running short, there may be the temptation to compromise quality in order to meet targets (and experience tells us this happens often). The sales manager who spends most of his or her time out of the office would not be a suitable candidate either, as the quality responsibilities in the factory could conflict with responsibilities in the field.

The management skills of a typical management representative would include:

- excellent interpersonal skills, and the ability to communicate well at all levels;

- single-minded approach to long-term projects and working to deadlines;
- sound problem-solving abilities;
- good leadership, motivation and delegation skills.

STRUCTURE OF QUALITY SYSTEMS TO BS EN ISO 9000

In the example in chapter 1 of the basic quality system in a sales and despatch office, it was stated that quality systems may be properly documented, written on pieces of scrap paper, or in individuals' heads, and their chances of being effective depended much on the permanence of their recording, among other things. BS EN ISO 9000 leaves very little to chance in this respect. All aspects of the quality system must be fully documented, clearly and efficiently, and communicated to all on a need-to-know basis. As we delve deeper into the specific requirements of the Standard in section B, we will see that there must also be procedures for review, maintenance and updating of the systems and documentation.

The structure of the systems documentation follows the pattern shown in Fig. 3.2.

The quality manual

The quality manual includes the organisation's quality policy and addresses each of the requirements of BS EN ISO 9000 in broad terms related to the activities of the organisation. There is little detail (this is given in the other documentation), but the quality manual is used to show customers, staff, and anyone else who needs to know how the organisation goes about the achievement of its quality objectives, especially in relation to BS EN ISO 9000.

Procedures manuals

Each function or department will have its own procedures manual in which the procedures related to quality operations of that department are detailed. These manuals are much more specific than the quality manual, and therefore contain much more detail. For example, although a factory will have only one quality manual, it may have separate procedures manuals for design and development, raw materials warehousing,

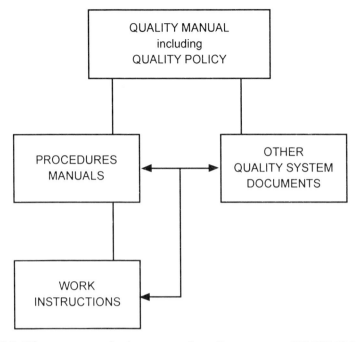

Fig. 3.2   The structure of a documented quality system to BS EN ISO 9000

production, planned maintenance, inspection and test, non-conforming product, etc.

Work instructions

Work instructions will be referred to in the procedures manuals, and will give precise details of how individual operations are to be carried out to enable them to be performed to the required quality. They will be sited at the appropriate point on the shop floor, or with the personnel carrying out the operations, and may be purely text, or refer to drawings or examples/standard models, etc.

Other documentation

There will need to be other documents supporting the quality system, e.g. inspection reports, lists of approved suppliers, non-conforming product reports, training records, and so on.

Examples of formats for the quality manual, procedures manuals and work instructions, together with representative samples of much of the other documentation for an approved quality system, will be found in section C of this book.

SUMMARY

- The correct motivation is essential when seeking accreditation to BS EN ISO 9000. Strategic, customer- and market-based motives are most likely to to bring success.
- Commitment is also necessary. This must come from the top of the organisation, extend to all personnel, and continue indefinitely.
- The organisation must be customer-orientated and all staff need to become fully involved. There needs to be a management representative for quality with no conflicting responsibilities.
- The quality system must be documented and structured in line with the requirements of BS EN ISO 9000.

In the next chapter we shall begin to look at the preparation and planning required to gain accreditation to BS EN ISO 9000.

4

PREPARATION AND PLANNING FOR BS EN ISO 9000 ACCREDITATION

THE ACCREDITATION PROCESS

Before being registered as BS EN ISO 9000 approved, an organisation's quality system must itself be approved and the organisation assessed to ensure that the system can be seen to be fully effective. This approval and assessment must be carried out by one of the many approval bodies established specifically for this purpose. The process is summarised diagramatically in Fig. 4.1.

Scope

Having decided which part of BS EN ISO 9000 the organisation wishes to seek accreditation to, and which areas of its activity it wants accredited, the first step is to identify one or more potentially suitable approval bodies. (These are discussed further later in this chapter.)

Initial discussion and questionnaire

The selected approval body or bodies will require a questionnaire to be completed, with details of the organisation, typically:

- whether the organisation is part of a larger one;
- the number of sites coming within the scope of the quality system;
- the number of employees;
- the products and/or services provided;
- the current status of quality systems, if any;

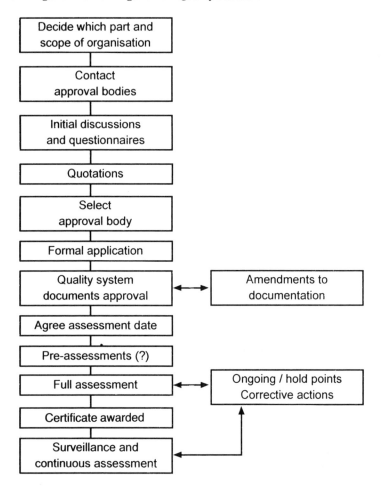

Fig. 4.1   The BS EN ISO 9000 accreditation process

● the part of BS EN ISO 9000 to which the organisation is seeking
  accreditation.

This questionnaire could well be combined with a visit from an adviser
from the approval body who will be able to answer any questions relevant
to the approval process, and the part that his or her body can play.

Quotation

After the questionnaire has been dealt with the approval body or bodies will be able to specify the fees payable for registration and assessment, both for approval purposes and for continued surveillance and periodic reassessment. The costs will depend on the parameters described in the questionnaire. Generally, the larger the organisation the higher the fees, particularly in the case of a multi-site operation. BS EN ISO 9001 will incur higher costs than 9002, which in turn will be more costly than 9003.

Application

Once the most suitable approval body has been selected, formal application for registration to BS EN ISO 9000 can be made, and the fees for registration and assessment would normally be payable at this stage.

Quality system approval

When the documented system is in an advanced state of development, it will be examined by the approval body. Although all the systems will not be complete, the quality manual must be approved, following amendment if necessary. At this stage, most organisations will be in a position to agree suitable timescales for completion of work on the development and implementation of the complete system and the date for full assessment.

Pre-assessments

At any stage, the organisation may have a pre-assessment carried out by the approval body or an independent third party. This will help to ensure that the system is developing on the right lines, but it will be charged for by the assessor. (Part of the intention of the Audit System in section B of this book is to reduce the need for pre-assessments.)

Assessment

At the appointed time, the approval body will make a thorough assessment of the organisation's quality system, auditing in great depth its suitability to the organisation and conformance to the requirements of the Standard. The assessors will be looking for evidence that the systems are being applied throughout the organisation and are proving to be effective. No stone is likely to be left unturned and any staff member may be called upon by the assessors to demonstrate his or her role in relation to the quality system.

The assessment could take anything from a few hours to several days, according to the size and scope of the organisation. Each site where the quality system is in place may be visited. There are four possible outcomes of the assessment.

Pass

The assessors will find no fault with the quality system and will be completely satisfied that the system and its implementation and effectiveness comply totally with the requirements of the Standard. A recommendation to award a certificate of registration will be made.

Ongoing non-conformities

Although the quality system and its implementation and effectiveness for the most part conform with the Standard, one or more minor deficiencies will need attending to. These will be insufficient to prevent the assessors' recommendation of the award of the certificate, but will be examined for the appropriate corrections during subsequent surveillance visits.

Hold points

One or more serious non-conformities will be found which show that the system, or its implementation, does not meet the requirements of the Standards. The award of the certificate will not be recommended, but the organisation will be given the opportunity, during an agreed timescale, to put right the deficiencies. The assessors will return to re-examine those areas subject to the hold, and, if satisfactory, will pass the system for the certificate to be awarded.

Fail

The system will fail to meet the requirements in a substantial number of areas. The assessors will discuss the appropriate course of action to be followed with the organisation, which may be complete or partial redevelopment of the system or abandonment.

Award of certificate

Following the recommendations of the assessors, the appropriate certificate will be issued. The organisation may then legitimately and proudly display it, and claim to be an organisation registered to the

Standard and display the 'Approved' logo on its premises, stationery and publicity material.

Surveillance and continuous assessment

The registration will be valid initially for three years, during which time the approval body will make periodic surveillance visits and carry out spot checks to ensure that the quality systems continue to be developed and implemented effectively, and that any ongoing non-conformities raised previously have been attended to. After three years a full assessment will again take place to determine if continued registration is appropriate.

THE WORKING PARTY

Most organisations will set up a working party or steering group to perform a feasibility study and the groundwork to present to senior management prior to getting down to the detailed planning of the project. It should include the quality representative if he or she has been nominated, and its objects will include selecting the approval body, examining the requirements of BS EN ISO 9000 in relation to the current systems in place in the organisation, evaluating the possible benefits that accreditation will bring, and estimating the costs of implementing quality systems and registration. At this stage it is likely that only budget figures will be available for benefits and costs, and commitments made now of finance and personnel should be regarded as provisional only. As will be seen in the detailed planning stage, until the size of the total project has been fully determined, it will not be possible to estimate with any accuracy the resources required.

SELECTING AN APPROVAL BODY

In England over 40 approval bodies are licensed for the certification of organisations to BS EN ISO 9000 Standards; a full list of names and addresses is included in section D at the end of this book. Some are specialists in certain fields (e.g. engineering, electrical industry, concrete, etc.), and care should be exercised in selecting the one most appropriate for the organisation. As with choosing any supplier, you should contact several, seek their advice and obtain quotations for their services. Your choice will depend on their expertise and experience in your type of operations, and their ability to provide you, the customer, with the quality of service you require. Talking to other organisations or trade associations in your field who have had dealings with approval bodies will help.

THE IMPORTANCE OF EFFECTIVE PLANNING

The development and implementation of quality systems, and the process of having those systems approved to BS EN ISO 9000 standards, must be considered a major medium- to long-term project for any organisation. As with any project, effective planning is vital. Time spent on the planning stage is seldom wasted and is likely to pay dividends in avoiding mistakes and costly back-tracks. The best result of a lack of, or inadequate, planning is likely to be chaos, and at worst it could lead to total failure. Good planning will enable objectives to be achieved within agreed timescales, and provide reference points for performance assessment along the way, allowing deficiencies to be identified, measured and corrected before they cause major obstacles to progress.

A good plan will have:

- clear objectives;
- an established starting point and knowledge of existing resources;
- assessment of additional resource requirements;
- identified priorities;
- allocated tasks;
- defined timescales;
- means of monitoring performance.

It should evolve from research and discussion with all involved in its implementation, and be agreed, written down and communicated to all parties concerned. The original working party/steering group is now likely to change its membership as necessary to become a project planning group.

Objectives

These should state clearly what the outcome of the project is expected to be, for example which part of the Standard is being sought and which areas of the organisation are to be included. Is it a case of aiming for BS EN ISO 9002, with BS EN ISO 9001 to follow later? Are all the functions of the organisation to be included in the scope of the registration in the first place, or will some be included at a later date, or never? What about the need to maintain accreditation after the event? The more specific the objectives, the less is left to chance and/or speculation, and the more comprehensive and workable the plan will be.

The starting point

Many an otherwise good plan can fail because those involved have not been aware of the point from which it starts. How can we expect to determine how to get from A to B if we don't know precisely where A is? To establish the starting point, we need to consider the following matters.

Existing systems and procedures

This is one of the key areas in assessing the size of the project, and therefore the timescales and requirements for resources. What systems are in place currently that may at least partly conform with the requirements of BS EN ISO 9000? It is well worth spending some time on a thorough investigation into how closely present operations do or do not meet the Standard. This is a major purpose of the comprehensive audit system in section B of this book, and this opportunity should be taken to make the first of possibly many such audits of the organisation. In this way estimates of the amount of work that needs to be done in each area of the organisation can be made prior to tasks and sub-projects being allocated.

Personnel

Which staff are available to devote extracurricular activity to the development and implementation of quality systems? How much time will they have available? Will secretarial staff be able to take on the extra burden of typing manuals and procedures, etc.? Are there suitably skilled people from relevant departments in or reporting to the project team to direct the proceedings? If one has not already been nominated, is there a manager who could take the position of quality representative? Is the local college or university able to assist with out-placements of students?

Knowledge and expertise

Questions raised regarding personnel resources available will also prompt an examination of the available knowledge and expertise in the organisation. Is there anyone with experience of setting up quality systems or working to BS EN ISO 9000 requirements? Are there the training abilities to enable new skills to be taught? Has anyone attended any relevant courses? Are the skills, knowledge and/or qualifications available in another branch, or another member of the same group? Can the local college or university help again?

Finance

Has any cash been allocated for this project in the budget? If not, is there any money in another area, for example an amount set aside for development that could be allocated? What grants are available in this geographical area and/or for this type of organisation that can be applied for? Does the local TEC offer assistance? (For possible sources of information about grants and TEC assistance, refer to addresses in the appendices in section D at the end of this book.)

Other resources

Is there spare office space which could be used for the project: desk(s), filing cabinets, a spare typewriter/word processor? Is the local TEC offering assistance, workshops, group schemes, subsidised consultancy, etc., that we can make use of? Does the local university or college provide help by the out-placement of students for work experience?

Resources required

Having established the objectives, and the size of the project using the audit system, the resources available can be allocated. It is quite likely that there will be a shortfall in one or more areas; the key to successful planning here is to make as accurate as possible forecasts of the levels of additional resources required. It is likely to have to review the resource requirement continually throughout the planning stage. Consider the following.

People

Along with people must be considered the knowledge and expertise required. Much time will need to be spent in all departments in developing the quality systems and their documentation; this is best done by those who carry out the tasks being documented, with specialist help as needed. This could result in their attention being diverted from their regular work for long periods. If the manpower and skills already available are insufficient for the project, it follows that assistance will have to be brought in. Here, decisions will have to be made between permanent employees (entailing a continuous commitment in terms of salaries and other employment costs) and temporary help, such as agency staff and/or consultants, who, although probably costing considerably more on an hourly or daily basis, can be used only as required. Much will depend on the type of skills required; for example, it may be considered necessary to employ the services of someone with expert knowledge of BS EN ISO 9000 and the implementation of quality systems for the odd day or two here and there to advise on and confirm the work in progress, but a typist may be needed on a more regular basis, even permanently.

Materials and equipment

It may be possible to purchase stationery through existing budget allocations, but it must be borne in mind that the requirement for paper, binders, folders, etc. will be quite considerable for the manuals and documents that will be written – and possibly rewritten many times – during the course of the project. In addition, the equipment and space necessary for production and storage of the documentation must be provided if not already available.

Finance

All the additional resources described above will need to be funded, as will the one-off and ongoing costs of registration and assessment by the approval body, and, hopefully, the provision of new stationery and promotional material to tell the world that you are now an accredited organisation. It is important to calculate the figures as accurately as possible during the planning stage, to avoid the danger of funds running out during the project. Finally, don't forget to budget for a massive staff party to celebrate the acquisition of the certificate!

It is important not to underestimate the various resources needed.

Indeed, one of the requirements of BS EN ISO 9000 is that management must provide sufficient resources to develop, implement and maintain the quality systems; once resources have been allocated, it may be extremely difficult or impossible to obtain more part-way through the project.

Identifying priorities

One of the benefits of the audit system is that, as well as enabling you to measure the overall size of the project, by splitting it into many small parts it can highlight the amount of work required in individual areas of the business. Clearly, some of these sub-projects will be much larger than others, requiring more time and attention. It is important to identify those requiring more work as they will need to be started earlier if timescales are to be adhered to – remember that the minimum time in which a project can be completed is the length of time it takes to complete the longest component. Another thing that may come to light as a result of the audit is one or more deficiencies in the organisation which can be rectified quickly and provide a dramatic benefit. Give anything such as this a high priority: correcting it demonstrates to the whole organisation that quality systems work. There is nothing quite like a quick break-through to give inspiration and boost morale, and if it has a positive effect on customers or leads to a cost saving, the impact on the organisation could be tremendous.

Allocating tasks

Having identified tasks and priorities it is necessary to decide on actions to complete them. This means determining the 'What?', 'Who?', 'Where?', 'How?' and 'When?' in relation to each sub-project; fitting the people and resources to the tasks. It may be necessary to review and modify the resource requirement during this process, but until all these open questions can be answered for each task, the planning is not complete.

Timescales

The timescale for the overall project cannot be set until all (or most) of the unknowns are resolved. For example, it will be impossible to predict how long the project will take until the starting point, the existing resources and the extent of the work required have all been established, and the additional resource requirement estimated and provided for. It is imperative to set a rigid timescale, however, as what tends to happen in practice is that the project will drift on and on as other priorities come and go. Since no definite completion date has been set no harm can be done by delaying it. Fortunately, with BS EN ISO 9000, the assessment date is a natural deadline; therefore setting the date early on will help by giving a definite target to work to.

Frequently a little 'juggling' with resources and timescales is needed; if working to a fixed budget which is patently inadequate, extending the timescales may help by, for example, reducing the need for external assistance. Conversely, increasing the resources available could help to shorten the time taken to complete the project. Beware of trying to rush it through, however; it is necessary to demonstrate to the assessors a history of effective implementation! The most important aspect of the time factor is to plan it carefully, set some realistic timescales for assessment and all the sub-projects on the way – and stick to the plan.

Monitoring performance

How do you know, part-way through the project, if you are on target? How do you avoid the eleventh-hour panic that usually occurs in the final weeks leading up to assessment, when procedures still have to be written, training has not taken place, and the quality manager is tearing his or her hair out trying to get the whole thing together in time? The answer is to build frequent reviews into the plan. Bearing in mind that the project as a whole will include very many sub-projects, each should be treated as the main one, with objectives, starting points, resource allocation, timescales, etc. These individual tasks should be fitted into the overall plan, paying particular attention to questions such as whether they can be carried out concurrently or must be consecutive, whether one depends on completion of another, whether there will be conflicts in the requirements for people or other resources, etc. It helps to commit the plan to paper to show graphically how each sub-project fits into the overall scheme.

Reviews should be held regularly with all concerned to look at what has been accomplished, what went well or badly and how well timescales have been adhered to. If necessary, work patterns or timescales can be adjusted to bring things back on schedule and all can learn from the experience. If small corrections are continually being

● Appoint a quality representative.

● Form a working party/steering group:
    Establish motivation for seeking accreditation.
    Evaluate benefits of accreditation.
    Decide appropriate part of BS EN ISO 9000.
    Decide scope of organisation for accreditation.
    Contact approval bodies, obtain information and quotations.
    Conduct audit (as per section B of this book).
    Evaluate existing resources:
        finance;
        personnel;
        expertise.
    Estimate approximate costs:
        approval body fees for registration and assessment;
        costs of additional resources required:
            finance;
            personnel and expertise;
            materials and equipment;
        commitment and culture costs.

● Present results of feasibility study, confirm motivation, make decision to go ahead on principle.

● Bring additional expertise to steering group to form planning group:
    Re-establish existing conditions (systems, etc.).
    Re-establish existing resources.
    Make detailed schedules of tasks.
    Evaluate in detail additional resources required:
        finance;
        personnel and expertise;
        materials and equipment.
    Identify priorities in plan – look for:
        possibilities for a quick breakthrough;
        long sub-projects that may determine ultimate timescales.
    Decide the What?, Who?, Where?, How?, When? for individual tasks and groups of tasks.
● Define timescales for:
    quality system documents review;
    pre-assessments;
    final assessment.

● Present results of planning, get firm commitment to project and approval on resources.

● Select approval body.

● Make application for registration.

● Put plans into action, with regular reviews.

Fig. 4.2   Checklist for planning accreditation

made and individual targets being met, the ultimate target will easily be met.

Figure 4.2 provides a checklist, drawing together the matters discussed in this chapter.

SUMMARY

- The accreditation process involves the review of the documented quality system, followed by an in-depth assessment of the system, its implementation and effectiveness. On satisfactory completion of the assessment a certificate of conformance to BS EN ISO 9000 will be awarded.
- Accredited organisations will be subjected to ongoing surveillance and assessment by the approved body.
- It is usual for a working party to be formed to examine the relevance of BS EN ISO 9000 to the organisation and the benefits and costs of accreditation.
- The selection of the approval body is made by the organisation with regard to its suitability and experience in the relevant fields.
- For the best chance of success in what is a long-term project, detailed planning is vital, taking into account the objectives, the starting point, resources available and required and their allocation, and timescales.
- Continual monitoring of performance is necessary to complete the project within the timescales.

Before we look in detail at the requirements of BS EN ISO 9000 in section B of the book, the next chapter looks generally at auditing systems.

5

QUALITY AUDITS

The whole subject of audits is vast and generally beyond the scope of this work. Many books have been written on audits, auditing and auditors, and courses and qualifications are available for those wishing to study the subject in depth. The following notes on audits and their conduct have been included because of their importance in the implementation and maintenance of quality systems to BS EN ISO 9000, and the fact that the major part of this work is centred on an audit system designed to aid the speedy, cost-effective and efficient development and maintenance of quality systems which conform to the Standard.

Quality audits were little known until the development of quality systems following the introduction of the Defence Standards but, with the increasing interest in BS EN ISO 9000, are becoming more common. A quality audit should be used as a management tool. It enables us to find out how well our organisation is functioning, and to identify areas in need of corrective action. For the purposes of quality systems, a good definition of an audit is:

An independent methodical study and review of one or more elements of a system, their operation, compliance with standards, results and effectiveness, for the purpose of verification and improvement.

Audits are involved in quality systems to BS EN ISO 9000 for a number of purposes:

- to establish a starting point for the development of quality systems;
- to monitor progress in the development of quality systems;
- to be a means of external assessment of the adequacy of systems for accreditation to BS EN ISO 9000;
- to provide statutory internal monitoring of the continued suitability, performance and effectiveness of systems;
- to assess an existing or potential supplier for its ability to provide goods and/or services of suitable quality.

THE SCOPE OF THE QUALITY AUDIT

A quality system audit will look for:

- *system adequacy* – whether the procedures are realistic and appropriate for the organisation;
- *system conformance* – whether the procedures are followed correctly on every occasion by all staff;
- *system performance* – whether the operation of the systems produces the required results.

An audit can rarely look in absolute depth at all aspects and details of the system (or part of one that is being audited). One of the keys to effective audits is to strike a balance between the 'broad brush' approach, which looks little more than superficially at the whole area being audited, and random in-depth investigations, where a small section is turned upside down and inside out. A combination of both is necessary in any one audit, the latter technique being used particularly if a problem or non-conformity is suspected.

GRADING THE RESULTS

The results of audits can be recorded in one of two ways. Sometimes it is a case of black and white: something clearly conforms or does not conform. For example, if the requirement is that a storeman signs a delivery note on receipt of goods, and goods are found in stock on the warehouse shelves with no signature on the delivery note, that is clearly a non-conformity. In other cases, several shades of grey could be involved to indicate a degree of non-conformity. If the storeman had instructed a junior member of staff to sign the delivery note, it could be regarded as a conformity in that signature was authorised by the correct person, but a non-conformity because the requirement specified signature by the storeman. In practice, at audit, this should reveal a grey area, and could well result in the quality system being altered to be more specific or more flexible, according to the needs of the organisation.

It is generally more useful to be able to grade a conformity/non-conformity than to view it in absolute black and white terms as it can identify the degree of seriousness of the problem and can often assist in allocating priorities for remedial action – obviously the more serious non-conformities will get priority. The audit system in section B uses a scale of 0 to 3, from not present at all to present and meeting the requirements totally.

INDEPENDENCE

One of the key words in our definition of a quality audit is 'independent'. A person cannot effectively audit his or her own department or operations. It would be too subjective; there would always be the temptation to pass the broad brush over areas of known or suspected non-conformity. Larger organisations employ permanent full-time auditors, but smaller ones use individuals with other functions, for example departmental managers or supervisors, to audit departments and functions other than their own.

TIMING

Should an auditor pounce unannounced on the auditee or should the audit be by appointment? It depends on the objective of the audit; if to catch someone out, for example to find evidence for dismissal of a member of staff, the unannounced pounce will be the better method. On the other hand, if the audit is to be conducted for the constructive purpose of ensuring that the organisation's systems are seen to be functioning, and as an aid to development, a planned audit schedule is to be preferred. This will be the case for the vast majority of quality audits; it gives the auditor and auditee the opportunity to prepare for the audit, and for it to be conducted with maximum co-operation on each side.

Subsequent audits of the same function or department should be arranged at different times of the day or week, especially if shift working is in operation, to ensure that audits will cover all aspects in due course.

POINT OF REFERENCE

All quality audits should be carried out against a specific point of reference; in most cases this will be the relevant section(s) of the quality system and clause(s) of BS EN ISO 9000. In this way there should be no possible argument about what conforms and what does not.

PREPARATION FOR AN AUDIT

Assuming that it is a planned quality audit, both the auditor and auditee should prepare well. The auditor should be familiar with the operations of the function being audited, the relevant quality systems, procedures and documentation in use, and the appropriate clauses of the Standard. He or she should prepare a checklist of areas intended to be investigated, along with questions to raise and operations and documentation that need to be seen. The topics of the audit should be chosen with care and relate to previous audits of the same department; it will be necessary therefore to consult records, especially if the auditor did not conduct the earlier audits. Areas which will warrant special investigation will include those not recently checked, those that were checked previously and found to be deficient, and those where deficiencies are known or suspected to exist.

The auditor should make the auditee aware in advance of the scope of the audit and specify what is expected of him or her. Auditees should make sure that their house is in order prior to the audit. This may seem to be defeating the object, but if the objectives are constructive, it will actually have a positive effect, prevention of non-conformities or deficiencies being better than cure. The auditee should allocate an appropriate amount of time to enable him or her to give full attention to the auditor. All staff should be made aware of the impending audit and their co-operation insisted on.

CONDUCTING THE AUDIT

The auditor and auditee should both endeavour to start the audit on time and stick to agreed timescales. The auditor should at all times be accompanied by a responsible person from the department, but be free to observe and question any member of staff.

Based on his or her checklist, the auditor must observe the operations, study the documentation and ask questions to determine whether or not the quality systems are being conformed to. Open questions should be used as much as possible: rather than 'Do you keep records of all inspection results?', it is better to ask 'How do you record inspection results?' followed by 'Where can I see them?'. Ask the What?, Why?, When?, How?, Where? and Who? questions, and when answered, confirm the answers with 'Please show me'. Do not restrict the questions to the auditee only but seek information from other members of staff. First-hand observations and questioning are essential. Get facts and see things for yourself; do not rely on hearsay. Make notes of your findings; memory alone is insufficient when summarising and producing a report.

Co-operation is vital for a successful audit. Both parties should avoid nit-picking, although auditor and auditee often disagree on what is or is not nit-picking!

At the end of the audit the auditor should sum up, and both should verify and agree the findings. Disagreements should be discussed and resolved. Any deficiencies found as a result of the audit must be identified, and the appropriate action to rectify them should be decided and agreed, with timescales. If appropriate, a date should be agreed to re-audit the deficient areas.

A report should be completed by the auditor (an example of an internal audit report is included in section C of this book) detailing all the findings of the audit, the deficiencies and actions agreed upon. The report should contain no new material other than discussed; there should be no surprises in the report for the auditee. Copies should be circulated as appropriate to the quality system.

THE QUALITIES OF A GOOD AUDITOR

Unless the organisation is large and can employ full-time auditors, many auditors will be part time and perform scheduled audits in addition to their normal duties. Auditing is a specialist function and the auditors will require specific skills and qualities. They should be selected with care, as with any employee, and be given the appropriate training. They need to be able to play the roles of both policeman and adviser, and the balance between the two is critical and will vary depending on the individual situation. They must be able to convey the purpose of the audit as being of benefit to the organisation and not a trial for the auditee.

Some of the qualities of a good auditor are:

- the ability to acquire quickly the knowledge and understanding of the function and associated systems being audited;
- independence; not to be swayed by pressure;
- the ability to relate well to people;
- the ability to act patiently, logically and professionally, and follow a course of action to a satisfactory conclusion;

- discretion;
- lack of bias.

Characteristics to be avoided are arrogance, being opinionated, impatience, gullibility and dishonesty.

The skills an auditor will need include the ability to:

- communicate;
- plan and control time;
- run effective meetings;
- gain co-operation;
- employ a systematic approach;
- lead and take control;
- earn respect.

THE ROLE OF THE AUDITEE

The auditee should remember that the audit is for the benefit of the organisation and not an appraisal of his or her personal abilities and performance. His or her department will benefit from efficient and effective systems and the audit should be a team effort to ensure that the requirements are satisfied and any possible improvements are made.

To enable the audit to be conducted efficiently and to produce the required results, the following tips are offered for auditees.

- Prepare; do homework – if possible, an audit should reveal no surprises.
- Advise staff of the impending audit. Tell them of its objectives and scope and seek their co-operation.
- Be co-operative; try to make the task as pleasant as possible for all concerned.
- Answer questions honestly; do not bluff and do not dig holes that you cannot climb out of! Do not attempt to hide known deficiencies.
- If a deficiency is found that can be rectified immediately, do it.
- Take notes to compare with the auditor's notes at summing up.
- Be assertive – challenge the auditor if you do not agree, but do not argue.

ASSESSMENT BY THE APPROVAL BODY

Pre-assessment checklist

As with any quality audit, thorough preparation on the part of the auditee, in this case the organisation, will pay dividends in helping to achieve a satisfactory outcome. All the rules given above for auditees apply here too, but a few extra follow.

- Ensure all staff are fully briefed as to the purpose of the visit.
- Ensure all areas are clean and tidy, good housekeeping is evident, and health and safety procedures are observed.
- Check that all written instructions and procedures are up to date and in place.
- Check that all quality records, inspection and test results and auditing documentation are up to date.
- Make sure that all measuring and control equipment is calibrated.
- Ensure that correct storage and labelling procedures are in evidence throughout the organisation, and that no unidentifiable material or product exists.

You will have no excuses; after all, you have planned and executed this project carefully and have probably had several months' notice of the date of assessment!

Assessment day

Unless an organisation is able to show commitment to the quality policy and procedures, from senior management to shop floor, the result of the BS EN ISO 9000 assessment will be 'fail'. One story often related, although never proved to be true, is of an approval body assessment team entering the building on the first day of assessment of a company. The lead assessor introduced himself to the receptionist, and asked her what the company's quality policy was. The result was a blank face on the part of the receptionist and an immediate 'fail' from the assessors for the omission of the company to implement such a small but vital element of its quality policy, in not making it known and understood by all employees!

During the assessment, an assessment team will examine in detail all areas of all functions and operations coming within the scope of the accreditation applied for, and any member of staff is a possible candidate for questioning; remember it is not just a case of Who?, Why?, How?, etc., but of 'Show me'. It is important therefore that all know what they are doing and why they are doing it, and can relate their work to the relevant documentation. The wrong answers or the wrong impression could result in at best a hold point or ongoing non-conformity, or at worst a fail.

In all probability the assessment team are not familiar with your organisation, products and services, methods of operating, technology or control procedures. It is therefore important to assist them as much as possible, giving them full co-operation as required. Prior to the start of the assessment, hold a meeting with them, also attended by the senior executive on site, the quality manager and other senior managers, and other key members of staff involved in the audit. The lead assessor will introduce his or her team and outline the assessment procedures and programme.

A few tips

- Specify clearly at the initial meeting the areas of the organisation to be assessed and ensure that the assessors have free access.
- Provide the assessment team with an office or room where they can discuss the assessment in private.
- Allocate a member of staff to accompany each member of the assessment team at all stages of the audit. This staff member should make notes of any relevant points arising during the course of the assessment for discussion later.
- When something arises during the audit which the assessor is unclear about (or is a clear case of non-conformity to the Standard), he or she will make an observation note. It is clearly an advantage if the accompanying staff member can deal with as many of these queries as possible as they arise, thereby keeping the number of observation notes to a minimum.
- Any assessment other than of a small organisation is likely to last several days. If the assessors do not suggest it, ask for a review meeting at the end of each day, when any deficiencies found can be highlighted. It may then be possible to correct non-conformities to the satisfaction of the assessors before the end of the assessment.
- Remember, the assessors are human! They are there to do their job as you are to do yours. Make every effort to make it a pleasant experience for all concerned, whatever the outcome.

SUMMARY

- Quality audits are a necessary part of quality systems, in particular regarding BS EN ISO 9000.
- A quality system audit will look for adequacy, conformance and performance.
- Audits must be conducted by auditors independent of the function of the auditee.
- Audits are conducted for the benefit of the organisation, not as a trial for the auditee.
- Auditors should have the necessary qualities, skills and training.
- Preparation and co-operation are key elements for a successful assessment to BS EN ISO 9000.

The first section of this book is now concluded. Section B follows, which is based on the audit system. It also includes a detailed breakdown of all the elements of BS EN ISO 9000.

SECTION B

6

THE BS EN ISO 9000
TOOL KIT AUDIT SYSTEM

INTRODUCTION

This section is the system of audit devised to break down the clauses of BS EN ISO 9000 into small, easily manageable pieces, and apply each to an organisation's existing operations and quality systems for the purpose of evaluation relative to the requirements of the Standard.

Anything large and complex, although daunting at first sight, will consist of very many small and individually simple components. For example, the world's most powerful computer is basically millions of very simple on–off switches. BS EN ISO 9000 is difficult and time-consuming to swallow – not to be attempted in one mouthful! – but, broken down into constituent parts, can be tackled with relative ease.

The audit system asks a number of questions (over 260 in the case of BS EN ISO 9001) of the organisation being audited. The answer to each is a graded yes/no. Depending on how far or near to the requirements of the relevant Standard the organisation's current systems are judged to be, based on the requirements and notes accompanying each question, the auditor can give a score in the 0 to 3 range for each. The questions are all very simple, and some will be answerable quickly and readily. However, many are likely to require a considerable amount of investigation before the appropriate score can be given.

Once the complete audit or section of the audit has been completed, for each section of each clause of the Standard there will be a total score to measure against the maximum possible. In this way, the areas and extent of outstanding work will be identified, and action plans to address these deficiencies can be devised, prioritised and implemented. As progress is made, the relevant section(s) can be re-audited and the change in the scoring towards maximum noted; thus improvements can be numerically monitored.

HOW TO USE THE AUDIT SYSTEM

Before you start

Firstly, it is necessary to schedule a fair amount of time. This is not something that can be accomplished in an hour or two, even in the smallest of organisations. In many cases the complete audit may take several days or even weeks of concentrated time, depending on the size and nature of the organisation, number of locations, co-operation of staff, and the number of people allocated to the task. However, someone with in-depth knowledge of the organisation, after studying the remainder of this section B, should be able to estimate the time likely to be needed.

Be aware of which part of BS EN ISO 9000 the organisation is to be audited against, and of the scope of the audit – for example, is design to be included? are statistical techniques? etc. This may render a number of sections irrelevant. You will probably find it beneficial to study this complete section of the book before making these decisions, if they have not already been made. The audit sections are as shown in table B.1, which gives the maximum scores for each part of BS EN ISO 9000. Deduct the scores for any section not to be included and you will have the maximum score against which your organisation will be measured.

The format of the audit system

Each page of the actual audit deals with either a whole clause of BS EN ISO 9000 or one or more sub-clauses, depending on the extent of the clause(s) in question. On the left-hand page, the 'Audit Guide', is a summary of the requirements as laid down by the Standard, followed by some notes, which give a practical interpretation with occasional tips and examples to clarify the requirements. Note that section 4.9, Process control, gives an extra two pages of notes on processes (page numbers 31A and 31B).

On the facing right-hand page is the 'Audit Checklist', the series of questions related to the clause or sub-clause(s) in question. Space is allowed for comments against each question, and the bottom of the page is for notes and action points for addressing the outstanding matters.

A complete set of A4-size masters of the Audit Checklist pages is available from the authors. These can be used time and again to make photocopied working documents, giving more space for written

Table B.1 Maximum scores for each section of the audit system
(Page numbers refer to Audit Guide and Checklist pages)

Section	Page nos	Section title	BS EN ISO 9001	9002	9003
4.1	1–5	Management responsibility	93	93	93
4.2	6–8	Quality system	42	42	42
4.3	9–12	Contract review	30	30	30
4.4	13–21	Design control	117	n/a	n/a
4.5	22–24	Document and data control	33	33	33
4.6	25–28	Purchasing	36	36	n/a
4.7	29	Control of customer supplied product	15	15	15
4.8	30	Product identification and traceability	18	18	18
4.9	31–32	Process control	48	48	n/a
4.10	33–37	Inspection and testing	69	69	69
4.11	38–39	Control of inspection, measuring and test equipment	51	51	51
4.12	40	Inspection and test status	15	15	15
4.13	41–42	Control of non-conforming product	39	39	39
4.14	43–45	Corrective and preventive action	33	33	33
4.15	46–50	Handling, storage, packaging, preservation and delivery	48	48	48
4.16	51	Quality records	27	27	27
4.17	52	Internal quality audits	24	24	24
4.18	53	Training	24	24	24
4.19	54	Servicing	24	24	n/a
4.21	55	Statistical techniques	12	12	12
Maximum total scores			798	681	573

comments, allowing repeated audits to be recorded and avoiding the need to write on the book pages. See the page following the introduction at the front of the book.

Scoring

The audit questions require a qualified or graded yes/no answer by way of a score between zero and three. In deciding the appropriate score, consider the area being audited relative to the requirements of the Standard and the notes on the left-hand page. In order to gain a maximum score in any one question, the requirements of the Standard must be addressed within your organisation's quality system, they must be seen to be in evidence, and be documented and recorded. Score therefore as follows:

0   No evidence of meeting the requirements at all.
1   Element present in some respects; documentation absent, inadequate or incomplete.
2   Element and documentation mostly complete, but not meeting the requirements in full.
3   Evidence shows the meeting of the requirements in full.

Scores are arbitrary – a score of less than three will not mean the same level of deficiency or amount of work needed to be done as in another area with the same score. What is important is the movement in individual scores, i.e. from 0 to 1, 1 to 2, 2 to 3, and the effect on the totals over a period of time, indicating the progress being made in individual areas and the project as a whole. An example of a completed checklist is shown in Fig. B.1.

A maximum score will give an indication that the quality systems are likely to be adequate to meet the requirements of BS EN ISO 9000, but this is not guaranteed. Advice from an approval body or other qualified, experienced and knowledgeable sources will confirm the actual situation.

Terminology

BS EN ISO 9000 refers to the body seeking accreditation as the 'supplier'; we prefer to use the term 'organisation', to avoid confusion with the organisation's suppliers. The output from the organisation is usually referred to as the 'product', but this applies equally to services as well as manufactured products. BS EN ISO 9000 also use 'product' to refer to raw materials and work in progress. The person or body for whom the product or service is provided is generally referred to as the 'customer', although the Standard frequently uses the term 'purchaser' – it has the same meaning. The quality system requirements are all contained in main clause 4; clauses 0 to 3 of the Standard are concerned with introductions, the scope of application, references and definitions.

GRAPHICAL REPRESENTATION OF AUDIT SYSTEM RESULTS

It can be helpful to display the results of the audit system graphically, especially when showing the organisation's workforce the progress being made; it is informative and helps to maintain interest and motivation. A suggested format for an organisation aiming for all sections of BS EN ISO 9001 is shown in Fig. B.2. The shaded areas show the current status of the quality system in each of the sections as a result of the audit; the diagram can be built on to indicate progress after each repeat full audit or sectional audit. When all the blank spaces have disappeared, the organisation should be ready for assessment by the approval body.

There is plenty of scope here for the quality manager with imagination – the ambitious could produce tailor-made graphics in glorious colour for each department or function!

AUDIT CHECKLIST

BS EN ISO 9000

4.1 MANAGEMENT RESPONSIBILITY

4.1.1 QUALITY POLICY

	SCORE	COMMENTS
Does the organisation have a quality policy:		
specifying objectives for quality?................	0 ① 2 3	*Not clearly specified.*
specifying commitment to quality?..............	0 1 2 ③	
Is the quality policy:		
relevant to		
the organisation's goals...........................	0 1 2 ③	
the customers' needs/expectations?	0 1 2 ③	
documented as part of the quality manual?	0 ① 2 3	*Documented, but*
published within the organisation?	0 1 2 ③	*Q.M. not written yet.*
known and understood by all personnel?	0 ① 2 3	*Many staff unaware of policy.*
part of induction training for all new personnel?	⓪ 1 2 3	
Are customers made aware of the quality policy as required?...	⓪ 1 2 3	

MAXIMUM SCORE 27   TOTAL SCORE *15*

OUTSTANDING MATTERS	ACTION BY – WHOM	WHEN

1. Quality policy to be amended at next management meeting. — *All Mgt.* — *10–5–95*
2. Bob Jones to include quality policy when drafting quality manual. — *R.J.* — *May 95*
3. Training dept. to devise and implement q. policy training for all staff and re-format induction programmes. — *G.J.* — *Induction training from May 95. All staff by end of June 95.*
4. Marketing dept. to produce a quality policy statement. Sales to distribute to existing customers. — *M.C.* — *by 31–5–95* / *S.H.* — *by 30–6–95*
5. Re-audit this section. — *J.W.* — *1–7–95*

AUDIT NO *1*   DATE *28–3–95*   AUDITOR *John White*   PAGE 1

Fig. B.1   Audit checklist: quality policy

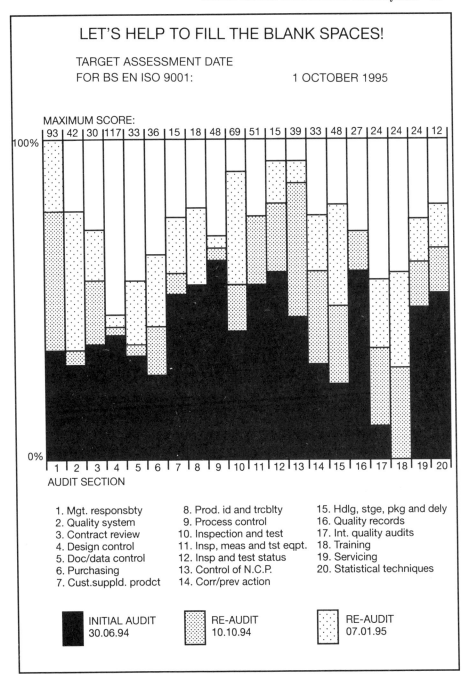

Fig. B.2   Graphic representation of audit system results

AUDIT GUIDE

BS EN ISO 9000

4.1 MANAGEMENT RESPONSIBILITY

4.1.1 QUALITY POLICY

QUALITY SYSTEM REQUIREMENTS

The organisation must define and document its quality policy in relation to its objectives and commitment. It must be relevant to the organisation's goals and the needs and expectations of its customers. The policy is to be published within the organisation, known and understood by all staff, and implemented throughout the organisation.

NOTES

Although generally a brief statement, the quality policy is the cornerstone of the entire quality system.

A typical quality policy may be on the following lines:

Summit Products Ltd's aim is to design, manufacture, supply and service road making and maintenance equipment to high standards, to enable the products at all times to be fit for their purpose.

It is the commitment of all the Company's management and staff to ensure that our products are supplied in accordance with our specifications and the agreed requirements of our customers.

In order to achieve these aims, Summit Products Ltd employs effective quality management systems that meet the requirements of BS EN ISO 9001, 1994.

Signed by_____Chairman & Chief Executive

Date_____SUMMIT PRODUCTS LTD

The quality policy must be relevant to, and published throughout, the organisation. It must be known and understood by all employees, not only as a statement, but with regard to its implications to the operations of the organisation. Therefore training in the quality policy for all staff, including new recruits, is essential (see also Training, section 4.18, page 53).

Customers are also entitled to know about the quality policy, and facilities should be available for them to be informed as required, for example, by means of a printed statement signed by a senior executive.

PAGE 1

AUDIT CHECKLIST

BS EN ISO 9000

4.1 MANAGEMENT RESPONSIBILITY

4.1.1 QUALITY POLICY

	SCORE	COMMENTS
Does the organisation have a quality policy:		
specifying objectives for quality?.................	0 1 2 3	
specifying commitment to quality?..............	0 1 2 3	
Is the quality policy:		
relevant to		
the organisation's goals?.........................	0 1 2 3	
the customers' needs/expectations?.......	0 1 2 3	
documented as part of the quality manual?	0 1 2 3	
published within the organisation?	0 1 2 3	
known and understood by all personnel?	0 1 2 3	
part of induction training for all new personnel?	0 1 2 3	
Are customers made aware of the quality policy as required?...	0 1 2 3	

MAXIMUM SCORE 27   TOTAL SCORE_____

OUTSTANDING MATTERS   ACTION BY – WHOM   WHEN

AUDIT GUIDE

BS EN ISO 9000

4.1 MANAGEMENT RESPONSIBILITY: ORGANISATION

4.1.2.1 RESPONSIBILITY AND AUTHORITY

QUALITY SYSTEM REQUIREMENTS

All those personnel in an organisation who have responsibility and/or authority for quality must be defined, in particular those who control and maintain the quality system, identify quality deficiencies in the processes and quality system, and control corrective actions and their effectiveness. Their responsibilities must be documented.

NOTES

Documented as part of the quality system, the structure of the management of the quality systems should be defined. In practice this would probably be a management structure diagram (see example of quality manual, section C), showing the lines of authority and responsibility for quality operations, not necessarily the same as for a functional structure. Individuals should be defined by function rather than by name, in case of future personnel changes.

In particular the following should be identified:

person with overall quality responsibility, i.e. a senior executive,

the management representative (and the person responsible for the implementation, maintenance and review of the quality system, if not the same),

those with key responsibility for:

purchasing materials and services,

control of processes,

inspection and testing of materials, in-process and final inspections,

initiating and following up corrective actions and effective actions to prevent recurrence of problems.

In order to make the responsibilities, authorities and inter-relationships clear, it may be considered helpful to include a brief job description for the key people, highlighting each's function related to quality.

PAGE 2

AUDIT CHECKLIST

BS EN ISO 9000

4.1 MANAGEMENT RESPONSIBILITY: ORGANISATION

4.1.2.1 RESPONSIBILITY AND AUTHORITY

	SCORE	COMMENTS
Does the organisation have a defined management structure which shows:		
managers with authority for quality?	0 1 2 3	
managers with responsibility for quality?	0 1 2 3	
inter-relationships with regard to quality?	0 1 2 3	
Is the structure documented as part of the quality manual?	0 1 2 3	
Does the structure show who is responsible for:		
identifying quality deficiencies?	0 1 2 3	
the control and maintenance of the quality system?	0 1 2 3	
the control of corrective action systems (see 4.14)	0 1 2 3	
effective corrective actions being taken? (see 4.14)	0 1 2 3	

MAXIMUM SCORE 24   TOTAL SCORE_____

OUTSTANDING MATTERS   ACTION BY – WHOM   WHEN

AUDIT NO_____ DATE_____ AUDITOR_____   PAGE 2

AUDIT GUIDE

BS EN ISO 9000

4.1 MANAGEMENT RESPONSIBILITY: ORGANISATION (cont.)

4.1.2.2 RESOURCES

QUALITY SYSTEM REQUIREMENTS

An organisation must provide the necessary resources, including trained personnel, for management, performance of work and vertification that the products and services are provided in accordance with its objectives for quality.

Verification includes the inspection, testing and monitoring of the design, production/processing, installation and servicing, and review and audit of the quality system to ensure its continued suitability and effectiveness.

NOTES

All management and staff involved in work that affects quality must be appropriately trained and qualified.

The organisation's product and services must have specifications for quality against which they can be measured. These specifications must relate directly to the parameters which give the quality characteristics of the products and/or services. For example, if a quality characteristic is an item's strength, which is dependent on its being a certain thickness, then that thickness must be one of the product's specifications.

Verification of quality will include the identification of the requirements for quality, inspection and test facilities and procedures (see Inspection and Testing, section 4.10, page 33 *et seq.*), and the means of monitoring all functions in relation to the effective working of the quality systems (see Internal Quality Audits, section 4.17, page 52, and section A, chapter 5).

All products require regular review of their fitness for the purpose; therefore testing the satisfaction/dissatisfaction of customers is important. Also the processes should be reviewed regularly and their continued suitability verified (see also Contract Review, section 4.3, page 9 *et seq.*, and Process Control, section 4.9, page 31 *et seq.*).

AUDIT CHECKLIST

BS EN ISO 9000

4.1 MANAGEMENT RESPONSIBILITY: ORGANISATION (cont.)

4.1.2.2 RESOURCES

	SCORE	COMMENTS

Does the organisation provide resources
and trained personnel to:

identify quality requirements?...................... 0 1 2 3

inspect and test products?........................... 0 1 2 3

monitor quality of internal services:
    design,
    production,
    installation,
    servicing? 0 1 2 3

independently audit systems, products
and processes? (see 4.17)......................... 0 1 2 3

review adequacy of systems, products
and processes?... 0 1 2 3

Can the existence of these resources
be verified? 0 1 2 3

MAXIMUM SCORE 18   TOTAL SCORE_____

OUTSTANDING MATTERS   ACTION BY – WHOM   WHEN

AUDIT NO_____ DATE_____ AUDITOR_____   PAGE 3

AUDIT GUIDE

BS EN ISO 9000

4.1 MANAGEMENT RESPONSIBILITY: ORGANISATION (cont.)

4.1.2.3 MANAGEMENT REPRESENTATIVE

QUALITY SYSTEM REQUIREMENTS

The organisation must have a member of its own management with the defined responsibility and authority for the implementation and maintenance of the quality system, its continued compliance with BS EN ISO 9000 requirements, and reporting on its performance to management for the purposes of review and continued improvement.

NOTES

Refer to section A, chapter 3, 'Management Representative'.

The key here is for the management representative to be free to undertake the responsibilities of the task without hindrance from any conflicting responsibilities. Although the management representative must take full responsibility for the quality system, it is permitted for tasks to be delegated.

Although not specifically required by the Standard, in practice it is necessary for the management representative to have a deputy, with delegated authority and responsibility, to act in his or her absence.

PAGE 4

AUDIT CHECKLIST

BS EN ISO 9000

4.1 MANAGEMENT RESPONSIBILITY: ORGANISATON (cont.)

4.1.2.3 MANAGEMENT REPRESENTATIVE

	SCORE	COMMENTS
Is there a nominated manager to represent the organisation on all matters relating to quality?	0 1 2 3	
Does he/she have a nominated deputy to act in his/her absence?	0 1 2 3	
Do they have the		
authority?	0 1 2 3	
responsibility?	0 1 2 3	

to ensure that the requirements of
BS EN ISO 9000 are implemented and
maintained?

MAXIMUM SCORE 12   TOTAL SCORE_____

OUTSTANDING MATTERS   ACTION BY – WHOM   WHEN

AUDIT GUIDE

BS EN ISO 9000

4.1 MANAGEMENT RESPONSIBILITY (cont.)

4.1.3 MANAGEMENT REVIEW

QUALITY SYSTEM REQUIREMENTS

Management must review the quality system at defined intervals to ensure its continued suitability and effectiveness in meeting the requirements of BS EN ISO 9000 and the organisation's quality policy and objectives. Records of these reviews must be maintained.

NOTES

These reviews may be held as part of regular management meetings, or, preferably, meetings may take place specifically for quality system review purposes. The frequency of meetings should be determined by the need; while systems are being developed this is likely to be greater than later on. However, it is important that reviews are scheduled and carried out at defined intervals, rather than held on an ad hoc basis.

Topics for review are likely to include:

the results of internal audits,

customer complaints,

specific quality system failures,

trends in non-conformities,

effects of corrective and preventive actions, etc. . . . . .

Records of reviews must be kept, which, for follow-up purposes, should include the allocated responsibilities of individuals to take actions decided, etc.

PAGE 5

AUDIT CHECKLIST

BS EN ISO 9000

4.1 MANAGEMENT RESPONSIBILITY (cont.)

4.1.3 MANAGEMENT REVIEW

	SCORE	COMMENTS
Are the		
suitability	0 1 2 3	
effectiveness	0 1 2 3	
of the procedures and policies reviewed at defined intervals by management?		
Are the results of internal audits regularly reviewed by management at defined intervals and in accordance with documented procedures?	0 1 2 3	
Are the reviews, and the decisions taken, minuted?...	0 1 2 3	

MAXIMUM SCORE 12   TOTAL SCORE _____

OUTSTANDING MATTERS   ACTION BY – WHOM   WHEN

AUDIT NO_____ DATE_____ AUDITOR_____   PAGE 5

AUDIT GUIDE

BS EN ISO 9000

4.2 QUALITY SYSTEM

4.2.1 GENERAL

QUALITY SYSTEM REQUIREMENTS

The organisation must establish, document and maintain a quality system in order to ensure that the product meets the specified requirements.

It must include a quality manual which references all the procedures and documentation related to the quality system.

NOTES

Refer to section A, chapter 1; also sample documentation in section C.

A quality system is an integral part of an organisation's management system, and describes the procedures used to ensure that the needs of the customer are met. It must also cater for the organisation's own needs and interests.

In the preparation of a quality system, an organisation needs to include the following:

A quality manual, approved and signed by the senior executive, which describes how the organisation addresses each of the requirements of BS EN ISO 9000, and the appropriate procedures and work instructions (see section A, chapter 3). Reference may be made to standard procedures in textbooks, but all procedures and instructions must be compatible with the products/services.

Identification of the controls, processes, equipment, skills and other resources that are utilised to meet quality requirements.

Details of the appropriate tolerances for measurements. This may be by reference to drawings, standards or textbooks containing standard procedures and tolerances, etc. Measurements that are subjective, for example, colour, feel (e.g. softness, smoothness, etc.), require special consideration and reference samples.

The means of keeping up to date with processes, inspection and test techniques, and other developments of relevance, especially when working with state-of-the-art developments.

Identification, preparation and maintenance of associated quality records (see section 4.16, page 51).

A quality system is unique to an organisation and cannot therefore be bought 'off the shelf'. It is necessary to make it only as complex as needed to fulfil its objectives; to prove that it exists, it works, and it achieves the desired results.

PAGE 6

AUDIT CHECKLIST

BS EN ISO 9000

4.2 QUALITY SYSTEM

4.2.1 GENERAL

	SCORE	COMMENTS
Is there a documented quality manual?...	0 1 2 3	
Does the quality manual define the structure of the quality system documentation?..	0 1 2 3	
Are all quality procedures included, or referred to, in the quality manual?...	0 1 2 3	
Is the quality manual laid out in a way that shows how the organisation addresses all relevant clauses of BS EN ISO 9000?	0 1 2 3	

MAXIMUM SCORE 12   TOTAL SCORE_____

OUTSTANDING MATTERS   ACTION BY – WHOM   WHEN

AUDIT NO_____ DATE_____ AUDITOR_____   PAGE 6

AUDIT GUIDE

BS EN ISO 9000

4.2 QUALITY SYSTEM (cont.)

4.2.2 QUALITY SYSTEM PROCEDURES

QUALITY SYSTEM REQUIREMENTS

Documented procedures must be prepared and effectively implemented as part of the quality system. The procedures must be in accordance with BS EN ISO 9000 and the organisation's quality policy.

The range and detail of the procedures must be in accordance with the complexity of the work and the methods and skills employed.

NOTES

Refer to section A, chapter 1; also sample documentation in section C.

Simple procedures may be incorporated in the quality manual, but it is more usual to establish separate procedures manuals covering various sections of the organisation, e.g.:

    Production procedures manual,
    Purchasing procedures manual,
    Inspection and test procedures manual,
    Calibration procedures manual,
    etc. . . .

In this way, the quality manual is a relatively straightforward document and does not need updating every time a procedure is changed. The quality manual will make reference to the appropriate procedures manual, e.g.:

    'In-process inspection is carried out in accordance with the Inspection and test pro-
    cedures manual, ITP-01, section 2.'

It is frequently difficult to determine how much detail to write into procedures. However, the detail only needs to be sufficient to convey in full and unambiguously to staff who are appropriately trained how the job is to be carried out. For example, a production procedure to weld together two pieces of metal need not go into details concerning welding techniques if operators who would be trained in welding skills are to be carrying out the process. However, the standard of training and/or skill level of the operators needs to be defined.

Procedures manuals and associated documentation need to be available for reference by all concerned with work described therein; i.e. production procedures must be available and accessible to people on the shop floor, purchasing procedures to those involved with all aspects of materials acquisition, etc. Unless confidential information is contained, procedures should also be available for reference by customers, if required.

As the quality manual makes reference to the procedures, the procedures must refer to any associated documentation, e.g. work instructions, drawings, specifications, etc., which should also be available for use by the relevant functions and staff.

AUDIT CHECKLIST

BS EN ISO 9000

4.2 QUALITY SYSTEM (cont.)

4.2.2 QUALITY SYSTEM PROCEDURES

	SCORE	COMMENTS
Are there documented procedures covering all relevant clauses of the Standard?	0 1 2 3	
Are the procedures consistent with the organisation's stated quality policy?	0 1 2 3	
Is the degree of documentation appropriate for the methods, skills and training levels of the organisation?	0 1 2 3	
Is the appropriate documentation available for reference by		
all company staff	0 1 2 3	
customers	0 1 2 3	
on a need-to-know basis?		

MAXIMUM SCORE 15   TOTAL SCORE_____

OUTSTANDING MATTERS   ACTION BY – WHOM   WHEN

AUDIT NO_____DATE_____AUDITOR_____   PAGE 7

AUDIT GUIDE

BS EN ISO 9000

4.2 QUALITY SYSTEM (cont.)

4.2.3 QUALITY PLANNING

QUALITY SYSTEM REQUIREMENTS

The organisation must define and document how the requirements for quality will be met within its quality system. The following, where appropriate, need to be considered in meeting the specifications for products and services:

the preparation of quality plans,

the identification and implementation of any processes, equipment, resources, skills, etc. necessary to achieve the required quality,

the compatibility of the design with all the other processes, including production, installation, servicing, inspection and testing, etc.,

quality control and inspection and testing procedures,

the development of measuring equipment, especially if this exceeds current state-of-the-art,

the appropriate stages of processes at which inspection and/or testing is to be carried out,

the definition of acceptable/unacceptable standards, whether objective or subjective,

the identification and preparation of quality records.

NOTES

The above list is not necessarily exhaustive; the key phrase here is 'where appropriate'.

Each organisation will have its own individual products and/or services which will have specific attributes by which quality can be measured. It is important at the design stage that these are identified; from there the development of the 'Quality Plan' for those products or services can begin; the position of the goal posts needs to be identified and documented at this early stage so that the game plan can be similarly recorded.

It is not necessary to have a documented procedure for quality planning, but there must be evidence that such planning takes place, e.g. minutes of a meeting, a checklist of criteria with how each is to be met, etc.

AUDIT CHECKLIST

BS EN ISO 9000

4.2 QUALITY SYSTEM (cont.)

4.2.3 QUALITY PLANNING

	SCORE	COMMENTS
Does the quality system define how the requirements for quality will be met?...............	0 1 2 3	
Are the key elements of fitness for purpose of the product(s) identified?...............	0 1 2 3	
Are the means to measurement of these key elements identified?..	0 1 2 3	
Does the system show how quality procedures will be:		
prepared?...	0 1 2 3	
implemented?	0 1 2 3	

MAXIMUM SCORE 15   TOTAL SCORE_____

OUTSTANDING MATTERS   ACTION BY – WHOM   WHEN

AUDIT NO_____ DATE_____ AUDITOR_____   PAGE 8

AUDIT GUIDE

BS EN ISO 9000

4.3 CONTRACT REVIEW

4.3.1 GENERAL

QUALITY SYSTEM REQUIREMENTS

The organisation must establish and maintain documented procedures for the review of contracts and the co-ordination of such activities.

NOTES

What the procedures must describe regarding contract review is detailed in the following sections (pages 10 –12).

In general, the procedures must be formal (documented) and identify those personnel responsible for contract review activities.

AUDIT CHECKLIST

BS EN ISO 9000

4.3 CONTRACT REVIEW

4.3.1 GENERAL

	SCORE	COMMENTS
Are there documented procedures to review all contracts?	0 1 2 3	
Are the personnel responsible for contract review activities identified?................	0 1 2 3	

MAXIMUM SCORE 6   TOTAL SCORE_____

OUTSTANDING MATTERS   ACTION BY – WHOM   WHEN

AUDIT GUIDE

BS EN ISO 9000

4.3 CONTRACT REVIEW (cont.)

4.3.2 REVIEW

QUALITY SYSTEM REQUIREMENTS

Before submission of a tender or acceptance of an order, the tender or contract must be reviewed by the organisation to ensure that:

the requirements are adequately defined (whether written or verbal) and are agreed before acceptance,

differences between the tender and the contract and/or order are resolved,

the organisation has the capability to meet the contract/order requirements.

NOTES

The organisation must not accept orders which it does not have the capacity or capability to fulfil. This means that the processes and methods, personnel and skills, and inspection and test techniques must be adequate to meet the requirements of the specifications. This is particularly important for a new product or service, or one that is bespoke.

All orders must have all the details affecting the quality of product or service in writing; this may refer to catalogues or brochures, etc. where these exist and give the necessary product specifications.

Although not a specific requirement of the Standard, the organisation should define the point at which an order is accepted (e.g. when the contact is signed, or when the customer has confirmed a telephone order, etc.). Verbal orders may still be taken (over the telephone, for example). It is necessary to confirm the orders either verbally at the time of ordering, and/or in writing, so that any misunderstandings or errors can be resolved. If verbally confirmed, the details must be recorded.

Where contracts are tendered for, there is frequently a deviation in the tender in one or more areas. Such deviations or non-conformities must be agreed with the customer and confirmed in writing, before the order is accepted.

Details regarding quality are likely to include areas other than the product or service itself, such as quantities, delivery times, price, terms of payment, etc., and must therefore be specified.

In the case of repeat orders and on-going contracts, periodic reviews are necessary to ensure continued capability of the organisation to supply and perform to specifications.

PAGE 10

AUDIT CHECKLIST

BS EN ISO 9000

4.3 CONTRACT REVIEW (cont.)

4.3.2 REVIEW

	SCORE	COMMENTS
For each contract review:		
Is the point at which an order is deemed to be accepted defined?	0 1 2 3	
Are the requirements of all parties adequately defined and documented?	0 1 2 3	
Are any non-conformities to specifications or tender resolved?	0 1 2 3	
Are the capabilities of all parties to conform to the requirements ensured?	0 1 2 3	

MAXIMUM SCORE 12   TOTAL SCORE_____

OUTSTANDING MATTERS   ACTION BY – WHOM   WHEN

AUDIT GUIDE

BS EN ISO 9000

4.3 CONTRACT REVIEW (cont.)

4.3.3 AMENDMENT TO CONTRACT

QUALITY SYSTEM REQUIREMENTS

The organisation must identify in the contract review procedures by which contract amendments are made and the information transferred to other functions.

NOTES

In many organisations without effective quality systems, this is where things often go wrong! Changes in the contract are often agreed between the sales department and the customer without the information being passed on to those departments who will be fulfilling the contract.

This situation is addressed by the development and implementation of documented procedures describing not only the process of making contract amendments but the means by which the information is transmitted to all relevant parties.

PAGE 11

AUDIT CHECKLIST

BS EN ISO 9000

4.3 CONTRACT REVIEW (cont.)

4.3.3 AMENDMENT TO CONTRACT

	SCORE	COMMENTS
Are there documented procedures to identify how contracts are amended?..............	0 1 2 3	
Are the means of communication of amendments to the appropriate functions in the organisation clearly identified?	0 1 2 3	

MAXIMUM SCORE 6   TOTAL SCORE_____

OUTSTANDING MATTERS   ACTION BY – WHOM   WHEN

AUDIT GUIDE

BS EN ISO 9000

4.3 CONTRACT REVIEW (cont.)

4.3.4 RECORDS

QUALITY SYSTEM REQUIREMENTS

Records of contract reviews must be maintained.

NOTES

Refer to section 4.16, Control of Quality Records, page 51.

All contract reviews msut be documented and authorised by defined responsible personnel.

It is necessary to be able to verify that, in addition to the review having taken place, the appropriate people (whether customers or within the organisation) have been informed via the defined channels. Copies of memoranda, etc., concerned with contract reviews will therefore form part of the quality records.

AUDIT CHECKLIST

BS EN ISO 9000

4.3 CONTRACT REVIEW (cont.)

4.3.4 RECORDS

	SCORE	COMMENTS
Are records kept of all contract reviews?	0 1 2 3	
Are records kept of the communication of contract amendments to the appropriate functions in the organisation?	0 1 2 3	

MAXIMUM SCORE 6   TOTAL SCORE_____

OUTSTANDING MATTERS   ACTION BY – WHOM   WHEN

AUDIT GUIDE

BS EN ISO 9000

4.4 DESIGN CONTROL

4.4.1 GENERAL
(Not applicable to BS EN ISO 9002 and 9003)

QUALITY SYSTEM REQUIREMENTS

The organisation must establish and maintain documented procedures to ensure that the design of its products and services meets with the specified requirements.

NOTES

When a product or service is being designed, whether for mass provision to many customers or as a bespoke item for one, there must be procedures in place to:

produce detailed specifications in line with the requirements of the customer(s);

verify that the organisation has the capability of producing the product or service;

verify that the product or service will be controllable within the organisation's quality system.

This area is regarded by many designers, technologists and engineers as their 'sacred cow'. The intrusion of quality systems is often seen by them as pure bureaucracy which limits their creativity. Clearly, if this is the case, the problem must be resolved by effective communication and training.

PAGE 13

AUDIT CHECKLIST

BS EN ISO 9000

4.4 DESIGN CONTROL

4.4.1 GENERAL
(Not applicable to BS EN ISO 9002 and 9003)

	SCORE	COMMENTS
Are there established and maintained documented procedures to control and verify that product designs meet the specified requirements?..	0 1 2 3	

MAXIMUM SCORE 3   TOTAL SCORE_____

OUTSTANDING MATTERS   ACTION BY – WHOM   WHEN

AUDIT NO_____ DATE_____ AUDITOR_____   PAGE 13

AUDIT GUIDE

BS EN ISO 9000

4.4 DESIGN CONTROL (cont.)

4.4.2 DESIGN AND DEVELOPMENT PLANNING
(Not applicable to BS EN ISO 9002 and 9003)

QUALITY SYSTEM REQUIREMENTS

The organisation must plan each design and development activity. Plans must include descriptions of, and individuals responsible for, each activity, and be updated as the design evolves.

Design and design verification activities must have adequate resources and qualified personnel assigned to them.

NOTES

The management structure, responsibility and authority for design should be clearly defined (see Management Responsibility: Organisation, Responsibility and Authority, section 4.1.2.1, page 2).

Each design project should have a documented project plan including the following:

identification of responsibility for each activity;

the allocation of adequate resources and suitably qualified personnel;

procedures for verifying that designs meet the specified requirements;

procedures for updating the plan as the design evolves;

procedures for monitoring and control of the activities, including communication between design activities, timing and reviews.

Much of the discussion about planning for accreditation to BS EN ISO 9000 in section A, chapter 4 of this book is relevant to design planning.

The emphasis on design planning must be on the philosophy of 'Get it right first time' in order to avoid costly mistakes. This is particularly important where several activities are going on at once, where effective communication and co-operation are vital.

PAGE 14

AUDIT CHECKLIST

BS EN ISO 9000

4.4 DESIGN CONTROL (cont.)

4.4.2 DESIGN AND DEVELOPMENT PLANNING
(Not applicable to BS EN ISO 9002 and 9003)

	SCORE	COMMENTS
Is the responsibility for each design and development activity identified?	0 1 2 3	
Do design/development plans describe and reference these activities?	0 1 2 3	
Are design and verification activities assigned to qualified personnel?.....................	0 1 2 3	
Do design and verification personnel have adequate resources?	0 1 2 3	
Are plans updated as designs evolve?............	0 1 2 3	

MAXIMUM SCORE 15   TOTAL SCORE_____

OUTSTANDING MATTERS   ACTION BY – WHOM   WHEN

AUDIT GUIDE

BS EN ISO 9000

4.4 DESIGN CONTROL (cont.)

4.4.3 ORGANISATIONAL AND TECHNICAL INTERFACES
(Not applicable to BS EN ISO 9002 and 9003)

QUALITY SYSTEM REQUIREMENTS

Necessary organisational and technical interfaces between different design groups must be identified. Information must be documented, exchanged and reviewed regularly.

NOTES

See notes on page 14.

Important interfaces sometimes neglected are those outside the design department. Other functions in an organisation should be involved in the design process, for example, purchasing, production, engineering, etc., and good communication and regular reviews are essential.

AUDIT CHECKLIST

BS EN ISO 9000

4.4 DESIGN CONTROL (cont.)

4.4.3 ORGANISATIONAL AND TECHNICAL INTERFACES
(Not applicable to BS EN ISO 9002 and 9003)

	SCORE	COMMENTS
Are interfaces between different groups identified and defined;		
organisational?...	0 1 2 3	
technical?..	0 1 2 3	
Is interface information:		
documented?	0 1 2 3	
communicated?...	0 1 2 3	
regularly reviewed?.....................................	0 1 2 3	

MAXIMUM SCORE 15   TOTAL SCORE_____

OUTSTANDING MATTERS   ACTION BY – WHOM   WHEN

AUDIT NO_____ DATE_____ AUDITOR_____ PAGE 15

AUDIT GUIDE

BS EN ISO 9000

4.4 DESIGN CONTROL (cont.)

4.4.4 DESIGN INPUT
(Not applicable to BS EN ISO 9002 and 9003)

QUALITY SYSTEM REQUIREMENTS

The organisation must identify and document design input requirements, including any statutory and regulatory requirements, and formally review them for adequacy.

Ambiguous, inadequate or conflicting input requirements must be resolved with those responsible for providing the requirements.

Design input should take into account the results of contract review activity.

NOTES

The design input requirements, that is the information and specifications necessary prior to commencing a design, could come directly from the customer or be produced by another function within the organisation. They will include such features as specifications of the product or service in its completed state, the criteria for its performance, the situations in which it will be used, along with any critical measurements or parameters.

Any related safety or environmental hazards, and legislation affecting the product or service or its use should also be identified, and it must be shown how the product or service is to conform – the onus is on the design department to be aware of safety and other statutory requirements.

Before accepting the design input, which should take into account the results of the contract review processes, the design department should ensure it is complete and sufficiently detailed to enable the design process to take place. It should be reviewed with the originator and any problems resolved. Full documentation is essential throughout the process.

AUDIT CHECKLIST

BS EN ISO 9000

4.4 DESIGN CONTROL (cont.)

4.4.4 DESIGN INPUT
(Not applicable to BS EN ISO 9002 and 9003)

	SCORE	COMMENTS
Are design input requirements:		
identified?..	0 1 2 3	
documented?	0 1 2 3	
reviewed for adequacy?	0 1 2 3	
reviewed for conformance to applicable statutory requirements?	0 1 2 3	
Are incomplete, ambiguous or conflicting requirements resolved with originators?	0 1 2 3	
Are there procedures to take into account the results of contract review activity?.............	0 1 2 3	

MAXIMUM SCORE 18   TOTAL SCORE_____

OUTSTANDING MATTERS   ACTION BY – WHOM   WHEN

AUDIT NO_____ DATE_____ AUDITOR_____   PAGE 16

AUDIT GUIDE

BS EN ISO 9000

4.4 DESIGN CONTROL (cont.)

4.4.5 DESIGN OUTPUT
(Not applicable to BS EN ISO 9002 and 9003)

QUALITY SYSTEM REQUIREMENTS

Design output must be documented in a verifiable form in terms of its requirements, calculations and analyses.

It must meet the design input requirements and contain or reference acceptance criteria.

It must identify any characteristics that are critical to the correct and safe functioning of the design.

Design output should be reviewed before release.

NOTES

Design output consists of the drawings and documentation produced by the design department to enable the design to be produced. It must contain all the calculations and analyses used in the design process and the results of any reviews; it should show how it meets the requirements of the design input in every aspect.

It must show how the product or service can be verified as conforming to specification during and after production, that is, what the criteria for acceptance are, and what characteristics are vital to its safe and correct functioning. Such information is likely to include:

specifications for raw materials;

methods for in-process and final tests;

inspection and test criteria and tolerances, etc.

Information must also be given as to how the product is to be operated, stored, handled, maintained, etc. in order to preserve its characteristics.

As with design input, the design output documentation must be formally reviewed before release.

AUDIT CHECKLIST

BS EN ISO 9000

4.4 DESIGN CONTROL (cont.)

4.4.5 DESIGN OUTPUT
(Not applicable to BS EN ISO 9002 and 9003)

	SCORE	COMMENTS
Is design output documented in a verifiable form in terms of:		
conformance to requirements?.....................	0 1 2 3	
calculations and analyses?	0 1 2 3	
Does design output ensure that:		
design input requirements are met?	0 1 2 3	
acceptance criteria are referenced?............	0 1 2 3	
characteristics essential to the		
safety..	0 1 2 3	
correct functioning	0 1 2 3	
of the design are identified?		
Are design output documents reviewed prior to release?...	0 1 2 3	

MAXIMUM SCORE 21   TOTAL SCORE_____

OUTSTANDING MATTERS   ACTION BY – WHOM   WHEN

AUDIT NO_____ DATE_____ AUDITOR_____   PAGE 17

AUDIT GUIDE

BS EN ISO 9000

4.4 DESIGN CONTROL (cont.)

4.4.6 DESIGN REVIEW
(Not applicable to BS EN ISO 9002 and 9003)

QUALITY SYSTEM REQUIREMENTS

The organisation must conduct formal documented reviews of the design results at planned and appropriate stages of the design.

Participants at the reviews must include representatives of all relevant functions and other specialists as necessary.

Records of design reviews must be maintained.

NOTES

The Standard does not specify what the 'appropriate' stages of design are as far as reviews are concerned. However, in addition to the formal design input and output reviews, the organisation may consider it necessary to include other formal reviews. What is important is that these reviews should be planned as part of the design process, and that it is the results of the design that are under review. Thus it is not just a case of looking at the design itself but at all the criteria specified in the design input and how the design is shaping up relative to these. At the same time it will be useful to look forward to the design output stage in order that the design development process remains on track.

Clearly it is vital that the appropriate people take part in the design reviews, including not only the design team, but specialists from other relevant functions. These latter may well include customers and other internal or external experts.

As with design input and output, design reviews must be recorded.

AUDIT CHECKLIST

BS EN ISO 9000

4.4 DESIGN CONTROL (cont.)

4.4.6 DESIGN REVIEW
(Not applicable to BS EN ISO 9002 and 9003)

	SCORE	COMMENTS
Are design reviews planned and conducted at appropriate design stages?.........................	0 1 2 3	
Do review participants include:		
representatives of relevant functions?.........	0 1 2 3	
technical specialists, as appropriate?..........	0 1 2 3	
Are records of such reviews maintained?........	0 1 2 3	
MAXIMUM SCORE 12 TOTAL SCORE_____		

OUTSTANDING MATTERS   ACTION BY – WHOM   WHEN

AUDIT NO_____ DATE_____ AUDITOR_____ PAGE 18

AUDIT GUIDE

BS EN ISO 9000

4.4 DESIGN CONTROL (cont.)

4.4.7 DESIGN VERIFICATION
(Not applicable to BS EN ISO 9002 and 9003)

QUALITY SYSTEM REQUIREMENTS

The organisation must establish procedures to verify that design output meets the requirements of design input. Verification must be planned and documented.

NOTES

At first sight it may be difficult to appreciate the difference between design reviews (section 4.4.6, page 18) and design verification. Like design reviews, verification must be planned and documented, and take into account all the design input requirements. Reviews are likely to be incorporated in design verification but the latter go much further, typically by:

undertaking trials of the new design;

calculating results using alternative methods;

comparisons of the new design with similar proven ones.

The particular methods used will depend on the characteristics of the design.

With new designs, there is frequently the temptation to get them into production and on the market without sufficient testing and proving of the design. The result is often disastrous, leading to recalls, redesign and remanufacturing costs, with severe loss to an organisation's reputation and customer base. Effective design verification will prevent this.

PAGE 19

AUDIT CHECKLIST

BS EN ISO 9000

4.4 DESIGN CONTROL (cont.)

4.4.7 DESIGN VERIFICATION
(Not applicable to BS EN ISO 9002 and 9003)

	SCORE	COMMENTS
At appropriate stages of design, are verifications:		
planned?	0 1 2 3	
established?	0 1 2 3	
documented?	0 1 2 3	
Are competent personnel assigned to verify designs?	0 1 2 3	
Are controls in place to verify that design output meets the requirements of design input?	0 1 2 3	

MAXIMUM SCORE 15   TOTAL SCORE_____

OUTSTANDING MATTERS   ACTION BY – WHOM   WHEN

AUDIT GUIDE

BS EN ISO 9000

4.4 DESIGN CONTROL (cont.)

4.4.8 DESIGN VALIDATION
(Not applicable to BS EN ISO 9002 and 9003)

QUALITY SYSTEM REQUIREMENTS

The organisation must carry out validations of its designs to ensure that the requirements of the users are met.

NOTES

As between design reviews (section 4.4.6, page 18) and design verification (section 4.4.7, page 19), there are subtle but important differences between design verification and validation. Whereas design verification looks at how well the design meets the design input, validation determines how the design meets the requirements of the user. If the design input has been performed correctly, verification and validation will give similar results; however, the following should be considered:

design validation is a natural progression from verification. It would not be usual to test a design against the requirements of the user before going through the verification process;

validation is usually carried out on the finished product, perhaps by including customer trials. Verifications may be performed at several stages during the design development;

if there are many different uses for the product, validation should be carried out under controlled conditions for each such use.

Note the use in this clause of 'the user' rather than the usual phrase 'the customer'. Clearly, for a design validation to be successful and meaningful, the product or service must be tested in the ultimate operating conditions by those who have the qualifications and experience to use and evaluate it or, in the case of field trials, by the user(s) within the customer's organisation.

Design should be the subject of continual review, verification and validation even after it has been in production and supply for some time, to ensure continued conformance to specifications and the meeting of customers' requirements.

AUDIT CHECKLIST

BS EN ISO 9000

4.4 DESIGN CONTROL (cont.)

4.4.8 DESIGN VALIDATION
(Not applicable to BS EN ISO 9002 and 9003)

	SCORE	COMMENTS
Does design validation take place to ensure conformance to user requirements?	0 1 2 3	
Are the results of design validation documented?	0 1 2 3	

MAXIMUM SCORE 6   TOTAL SCORE_____

OUTSTANDING MATTERS   ACTION BY – WHOM   WHEN

AUDIT NO_____ DATE_____ AUDITOR_____   PAGE 20

AUDIT GUIDE

BS EN ISO 9000

4.4 DESIGN CONTROL (cont.)

4.4.9 DESIGN CHANGES
(Not applicable to BS EN ISO 9002 and 9003)

QUALITY SYSTEM REQUIREMENTS

Procedures must be established and maintained to identify necessary design changes, and for them to be documented, reviewed and approved by authorised personnel.

NOTES

Design reviews are from time to time likely to reveal the need for design changes. The design process is on-going; rarely is a product or service designed once and remains the same throughout its life-cycle. This is particularly true of more complex designs. Changes may be to materials, construction, functioning, production methods, etc., or to make use of developing technology or make the product more acceptable to the changing needs of the market and customers.

Having been identified as necessary or desirable, any design change must follow the process of the design itself; it must be fully documented and its input and output requirements must comply with the Standard. Changes should be reviewed, verified and validated to confirm that the product or service remains fit for its original (or updated) purpose, and that its other functions are not adversely affected by the changes.

The identification of the need or desire for a change itself must be controlled, and a procedure should be in place to allow for that. The persons with the authority and responsibility for approving and authorising changes should be identified.

AUDIT CHECKLIST

BS EN ISO 9000

4.4 DESIGN CONTROL (cont.)

4.4.9 DESIGN CHANGES
(Not applicable to BS EN ISO 9002 and 9003)

	SCORE	COMMENTS
Are there documented procedures for		
identification	0 1 2 3	
documentation	0 1 2 3	
review by appropriate parties	0 1 2 3	
approval	0 1 2 3	
of all design changes?		

MAXIMUM SCORE 12   TOTAL SCORE_____

OUTSTANDING MATTERS   ACTION BY – WHOM   WHEN

AUDIT NO_____ DATE_____ AUDITOR_____   PAGE 21

AUDIT GUIDE

BS EN ISO 9000

4.5 DOCUMENT AND DATA CONTROL

4.5.1 GENERAL

QUALITY SYSTEM REQUIREMENTS

The organisation must establish and maintain documented procedures to ensure that all documentation and data, both hard copy and electronic media, whether of internal or external origin, is controlled in accordance with the requirements of the Standard.

NOTES

Appropriate documentation is fundamental to an effective quality system, and procedures to control the approval, issue and updating of all documents and data should be in place. (See also sections 4.5.2, page 23, and 4.5.3, page 24.) This refers equally to hard copy paperwork and electronic media such as data stored on floppy and fixed computer disks. It will include the quality manual, procedures manuals and any reference material, work instructions, drawings, inspection and test specifications, etc. (See also Control of Quality Records, section 4.16, page 51.)

Organisations which have problems with the control of documentation often find that the main reason is that they have several overlapping systems; clearly it is necessary to co-ordinate and streamline all documentary procedures through one central function. To ensure relevance and accuracy, procedures and work instructions are best drafted initially by those people responsible for carrying out the operations being described. It is usually necessary, however, for final drafting to be at least co-ordinated by the quality manager or other responsible person in order to ensure uniformity and compliance with the requirements of the Standard.

Examples of some of the essential documentation are given in section C of this book, and some tips on document creation are given in the introduction to that section.

Some documentation and/or data is likely to be provided by the customer or other external source. This must be controlled in exactly the same way as that of internal origin.

PAGE 22

AUDIT CHECKLIST

BS EN ISO 9000

4.5 DOCUMENT AND DATA CONTROL

4.5.1 GENERAL

	SCORE	COMMENTS

Are there documented procedures to
control all documents and data

of internal origin?....................................... 0 1 2 3

of external origin?....................................... 0 1 2 3

relating to the quality system
and Standard, both

paper?... 0 1 2 3

other media? 0 1 2 3

MAXIMUM SCORE 12   TOTAL SCORE_____

OUTSTANDING MATTERS   ACTION BY – WHOM   WHEN

AUDIT GUIDE

BS EN ISO 9000

4.5 DOCUMENT AND DATA CONTROL (cont.)

4.5.2 DOCUMENT AND DATA APPROVAL AND ISSUE

QUALITY SYSTEM REQUIREMENTS

Documents and data must be reviewed and approved by an authorised person prior to their issue.

A master list of all quality system documents and data should be established and maintained showing the current revision status of each item, and be available for reference.

Relevant documentation must be available at the locations where correct operation is essential to the effective functioning of the quality system, and any obsolete documentation must be either removed or identified to preclude unintended use.

NOTES

It is important that all parties have access to the relevant documentation and data and are using the same up-to-date versions, so careful control is necessary. Documents need to be identified with issue numbers to indicate the current version, an issue date, and a signature of approval for issue.

There should be a master list of all documents, indicating the current issue (see our example in section C of this book). It would be a useful addition to indicate against each item those people who would officially hold a copy, making a circulation list in the event of changes.

When a document is issued following approval, it is necessary for it to be distributed to all concerned as quickly as possible and any documents rendered obsolete either removed from circulation, or, if it is considered necessary for them to be retained for reference, to be clearly identified as obsolete so that they cannot be inadvertently used. A system for signing for receipt of new and recovery of obsolete documents (or their marking as such) is advised.

PAGE 23

AUDIT CHECKLIST

BS EN ISO 9000

4.5 DOCUMENT AND DATA CONTROL (cont.)

4.5.2 DOCUMENT AND DATA APPROVAL AND ISSUE

	SCORE	COMMENTS
Are all relevant documents reviewed and approved by an authorised person prior to issue?	0 1 2 3	
Is a master list maintained of documents and data identifying the current revision status of each?..	0 1 2 3	
Is all relevant documentation available at locations where quality operations are performed?	0 1 2 3	
Are all obsolete/invalid documents identifiable as such and protected from unintended use?	0 1 2 3	

MAXIMUM SCORE 12   TOTAL SCORE_____

OUTSTANDING MATTERS   ACTION BY – WHOM   WHEN

AUDIT NO_____ DATE_____ AUDITOR_____   PAGE 23

AUDIT GUIDE

BS EN ISO 9000

4.5 DOCUMENT AND DATA CONTROL (cont.)

4.5.3 DOCUMENT AND DATA CHANGES

QUALITY SYSTEM REQUIREMENTS

Changes to documents or data must be reviewed and approved by the function that reviewed and approved the original, unless specifically designated otherwise. The review/approval function must have access to all relevant background information.

Where practicable the nature of the change should be indicated on the reviewed document or its attachments.

NOTES

Document and data changes should be reviewed and approved by a competent person or function; this usually means the one who approved the original.

It is helpful (and a requirement, where practicable) for the nature of the change to be indicated to show users how procedures or specifications, etc., have altered. This is usually accomplished by placing a vertical line in the margin against, or underlining, the revised section in a written document, or by a brief description in an appropriate location on a drawing. Alternatively, details of the change may be given on an attachment but reference to the attachment should be made on the document itself.

Documents can grow 'messy' after a number of changes; for example, written procedures can become difficult to follow and may become ambiguous, and drawings can become unclear and difficult to read or interpret. Although not a specific requirement of the Standard, a useful procedure is to rewrite or redraw and reissue documents before such problems occur. (Our sample quality manual in section C is an example of a document that needed to be reissued after a number of changes. Refer to the section introduction.)

AUDIT CHECKLIST

BS EN ISO 9000

4.5 DOCUMENT AND DATA CONTROL (cont.)

4.5.3 DOCUMENT AND DATA CHANGES

	SCORE	COMMENTS
Are all changes to documentation and data reviewed and approved by an authorised and competent person prior to reissue?................	0 1 2 3	
Are changes reviewed/approved by the originating function/organisation unless specifically designated otherwise?..................	0 1 2 3	
Is the nature of a change indicated on a modified document where practical?............	0 1 2 3	

MAXIMUM SCORE 9   TOTAL SCORE_____

OUTSTANDING MATTERS   ACTION BY – WHOM   WHEN

AUDIT NO_____   DATE_____   AUDITOR_____   PAGE 24

AUDIT GUIDE

BS EN ISO 9000

4.6 PURCHASING

4.6.1 GENERAL
(Not applicable to BS EN ISO 9003)

QUALITY SYSTEM REQUIREMENTS

The organisation must establish and maintain documented procedures to ensure that all purchased material and services conform to the specified requirements.

NOTES

'Purchased material and services' here refers to any product or service bought in by the organisation for use in any connection with any activity that is governed by the quality system. This would therefore include material for processing or for use in the processes, and such services required for the effective operation of the quality system, for example, specialist engineering, cleaning, calibration, etc. services.

The organisation must be able to ensure that such materials and services are at all times of the required and specified quality. This is most often done through the Inspection and Test Procedures (see section 4.10, page 33 *et seq.*). It is worth mentioning here that a common characteristic of purchasing organisations is that they do not request exact quality specifications from their suppliers; these should be provided either by the supplier or by the purchaser as a standard against which to measure the provided materials or services.

Before engaging a potential supplier, the purchasing organisation must assess its ability to provide materials and/or services. If the supplier has an accredited quality system (BS EN ISO 9000, for example), this in itself may be all that is required to satisfy the purchaser of the supplier's capabilities. Beware, however! It is necessary to ensure that the accreditation covers the the appropriate aspects of the products or services for the needs of the organisation. For example, if you are buying a component for which the design is critical, and the supplier is accredited only to BS EN ISO 9002 or 9003, extra assurances will be needed. This may well also be the case if the accreditation is limited in scope to a certain area of the supplier's business.

It will often be considered necessary to survey a potential supplier by audit or questionnaire to assess its suitability, in which case parts of this audit or a questionnaire based on the sample in section C of this book may be used.

A list of approved suppliers should be maintained by the organisation, and no material or service purchased from an unlisted supplier.

PAGE 25

AUDIT CHECKLIST

BS EN ISO 9000

4.6 PURCHASING

4.6.1 GENERAL
(Not applicable to BS EN ISO 9003)

	SCORE	COMMENTS
Are there documented procedures and resources to ensure that all purchased		
material	0 1 2 3	
services..	0 1 2 3	
conform to the specified requirements?		

MAXIMUM SCORE 6   TOTAL SCORE_____

OUTSTANDING MATTERS   ACTION BY – WHOM   WHEN

AUDIT NO_____ DATE_____ AUDITOR_____   PAGE 25

AUDIT GUIDE

BS EN ISO 9000

4.6 PURCHASING (cont.)

4.6.2 EVALUATION OF SUBCONTRACTORS
(Not applicable to BS EN ISO 9003)

QUALITY SYSTEM REQUIREMENTS

Subcontractors must be selected on their ability to meet the specifications in the subcontract, including specific quality requirements.

The organisation must define the type and extent of the controls exercised over subcontractors, depending on the type of products and/or services, the impact of the subcontracted products/services on the quality of the finished products/services, audit reports and records of previous performance.

Quality records of acceptable subcontractors must be maintained.

NOTES

To a large extent the notes on purchasing in general (page 25) apply to the selection of subcontractors.

As with suppliers of goods and services, subcontractors should be assessed for their suitability. This should be done prior to their engagement by comprehensive auditing of their business (although not a specific requirement of the Standards, it makes common sense!), and, if possible, by reference to their previous work for other parties. Again, consideration should be given to any appropriate quality systems in operation and accreditation to a quality standard.

Work given to subcontractors should be specified in writing in detail, agreed and understood by both parties, so that each is aware of exactly what is required. It is up to the purchasing organisation to define the controls that it will be necessary to exercise over the subcontractor; these will depend largely on the significance of the subcontractor's work in relation to the quality of the finished product or service.

The organisation must be able to show in its quality records (see section 4.16, page 51) that its subcontractors are continually assessed, based on their performance records, to ensure their continued suitability. A 'risk factor' grading system will be helpful in determining the frequency of such assessments.

A list of approved subcontractors should be maintained, and work given only to those on the list.

AUDIT CHECKLIST

BS EN ISO 9000

4.6 PURCHASING (cont.)

4.6.2 EVALUATION OF SUBCONTRACTORS
(Not applicable to BS EN ISO 9003)

	SCORE	COMMENTS
Are there procedures to approve subcontractors for their ability to provide materials and services to the required standards?..	0 1 2 3	
Are the type and extent of control over subcontractors defined?..........................	0 1 2 3	
Are there procedures for monitoring the performance of subcontractors?	0 1 2 3	
Are records maintained of the subcontractors and their performance against standards?	0 1 2 3	

MAXIMUM SCORE 12   TOTAL SCORE_____

OUTSTANDING MATTERS   ACTION BY – WHOM   WHEN

AUDIT NO_____ DATE_____ AUDITOR_____   PAGE 26

AUDIT GUIDE

BS EN ISO 9000

4.6 PURCHASING (cont.)

4.6.3 PURCHASING DATA
(Not applicable to BS EN ISO 9003)

QUALITY SYSTEM REQUIREMENTS

Purchasing documents must describe clearly the product ordered, including, if applicable:

precise details of type, grade, style, class, etc.;

the title or other identification, applicable issue of specifications, drawings, processes, inspection criteria, and other applicable technical data, including requirements for approval or qualification of the product, processes, procedures, equipment or personnel;

the title, reference and issue number of a quality system Standard to be applied.

The organisation must review and approve purchasing documents for compliance with requirements prior to issue.

NOTES

'Purchasing documents' generally may be interpreted as purchase orders, but may well include supporting documents such as suppliers' catalogues and specifications, and material or service specifications drawn up by the purchasing organisation.

It is necessary to be precise in every detail when purchasing materials and services so that there is no question about what is required. A written purchase order is essential, containing all the relevant data needed to establish conformance to requirements, or reference to sources of data, e.g. catalogues, specifications, etc. The order must be reviewed and signed by an authorised person before being released.

Verbal orders are permissible provided that they are accepted 'subject to confirmation' by a formal document.

If goods or services are being purchased with reference to a supplier's accreditation to BS EN ISO 9000 or a similar quality Standard, it is important to make reference to the appropriate clause in the purchasing documentation.

The purchasing organisation or its customers may demand assurances of conformity of purchased product to specification by means of a certificate, etc.

PAGE 27

AUDIT CHECKLIST

BS EN ISO 9000

4.6 PURCHASING (cont.)

4.6.3 PURCHASING DATA
(Not applicable to BS EN ISO 9003)

	SCORE	COMMENTS
Do purchasing documents specify precisely the product ordered?......................................	0 1 2 3	
Where appropriate, is reference made to the relevant specifications, drawings, technical data, etc.?.......................................	0 1 2 3	
Where appropriate, is reference made to the relevant section of a quality Standard?	0 1 2 3	
Are purchasing documents reviewed and approved by authorised personnel prior to release?...	0 1 2 3	

MAXIMUM SCORE 12   TOTAL SCORE_____

OUTSTANDING MATTERS _____ ACTION BY – WHOM   WHEN

AUDIT NO_____ DATE_____ AUDITOR_____   PAGE 27

AUDIT GUIDE

BS EN ISO 9000

4.6 PURCHASING (cont.)

4.6.4 VERIFICATION OF PURCHASED PRODUCT
(Not applicable to BS EN ISO 9003)

QUALITY SYSTEM REQUIREMENTS

(4.6.4.1 SUPPLIER VERIFICATION AT SUBCONTRACTOR'S PREMISES)
Where the organisation intends to verify purchased product at the supplier's premises, the former must specify the arrangements and method of release in the purchasing documents.

(4.6.4.2 CUSTOMER VERIFICATION OF SUBCONTRACTED PRODUCT)
Where specified in the contract, the organisation's customers have the right to verify that the purchased product meets the requirements of the specifications; this may be at the premises of the organisation or its supplier.

Such verification by the customer does not absolve the purchasing organisation from its obligation to verify the product, or prevent it from rejection if appropriate.

NOTES

Both these sub-clauses are similar in concept, detailing the requirements of the Standard in the case of a customer verifying (or inspecting) products on the premises of the supplier. In the first case the organisation is the customer of the supplier or subcontractor, and in the second case the organisation is the supplier to its customer.

Clause 4.6.4.1 refers to the occasional requirement or practice for an organisation to inspect a supplier's or subcontractor's product at the latter's premises prior to delivery. If this is to be the case, the details of the requirements for inspection and release of the product must be specified in the contract or order.

Clause 4.6.4.2 refers to the possible requirement in the contract for the facility for the organisation's customers to verify conformity to specification of materials or services purchased from them, either at the organisation's premises or those of their supplier or subcontractor. However, customer's verification does not absolve the organisation from its responsibility to make verifications itself unless this is by agreement, and the customer's verification is in accordance with the organisation's own quality system.

The above rather wordy explanations may be summed up as follows:

If a customer wishes to inspect or verify a product at a supplier's or subcontractor's premises, the details must be specified in the contract or purchasing documents. The customer's verification does not necessarily mean that the organisation is exempt from its own verification.

AUDIT CHECKLIST

BS EN ISO 9000

4.6 PURCHASING (cont.)

4.6.4 VERIFICATION OF PURCHASED PRODUCT
(Not applicable to BS EN ISO 9003)

	SCORE	COMMENTS
Where a purchased product is verified by the organisation at the supplier's premises, are the arrangements and method of release specified in the purchasing documents?	0 1 2 3	
Where specified in the contract, are customers given the opportunity to verify that the purchased product conforms to specifications?	0 1 2 3	

MAXIMUM SCORE 6   TOTAL SCORE_____

OUTSTANDING MATTERS   ACTION BY – WHOM   WHEN

AUDIT GUIDE

BS EN ISO 9000

4.7 CONTROL OF CUSTOMER SUPPLIED PRODUCT

QUALITY SYSTEM REQUIREMENTS

Where material is supplied by the customer, whether for incorporation into the product or a related activity, the organisation must establish and maintain documented procedures for its verification, storage and maintenance. Any such material that is lost, damaged, or otherwise unsuitable for use, must be recorded and reported to the customer.

NOTES

In many circumstances material supplied by the customer is used in an organisation's processes or related activity, for example, a customer may supply its own branded packaging labels.

Although one would expect the customer to provide material in keeping with its own quality requirements, the onus remains with the organisation to ensure that this material conforms to specified requirements. It should be treated as any other material with regard to its verification, storage and maintenance. In addition the organisation has the responsibility to account for the material to the customer, and records should be kept concerning its receipt, storage, use or other mode of disposal.

PAGE 29

AUDIT CHECKLIST

BS EN ISO 9000

4.7 CONTROL OF CUSTOMER SUPPLIED PRODUCT

	SCORE	COMMENTS
Are there documented procedures for the		
verification...	0 1 2 3	
storage...	0 1 2 3	
maintenance	0 1 2 3	
of material provided by the customer?		
Are records maintained of any such material that is unsuitable, lost or damaged?................	0 1 2 3	
Are there procedures for handling such unsuitable, lost or damaged material, including reporting to the customer?	0 1 2 3	

MAXIMUM SCORE 15   TOTAL SCORE_____

OUTSTANDING MATTERS	ACTION BY – WHOM	WHEN

AUDIT NO_____ DATE_____ AUDITOR_____   PAGE 29

AUDIT GUIDE

BS EN ISO 9000

4.8 PRODUCT IDENTIFICATION AND TRACEABILITY

QUALITY SYSTEM REQUIREMENTS

Where appropriate, the organisation must establish and maintain documented procedures to identify any product from drawings, specifications or other documents at any stage of production, delivery or installation.

If traceability is a specific requirement, individual products or batches must have a unique identity, which is recorded along with relevant data.

NOTES

All products, including raw materials, material in any stage of processing and completed products, should be readily identifiable. Although it is often sufficient to be able to relate the product to drawings or specifications, etc., to avoid confusion in practice it is often more satisfactory to employ systematic labelling. This could involve part-number or colour-code labelling on the product itself, or labelling on boxes of material, and is particularly important for items that could easily be mistaken or mixed up; for example, different sizes of the same article of clothing, light bulbs of different wattage, etc.

In some organisations it is essential to be able to trace materials or products after they have been sold; for example, in the food and drugs industries it is necessary to batch-code products in case of later problems. In such cases relevant production information (e.g. batch numbers of raw materials, date of production, line or process number, shift number, etc.) should be recorded against each batch number, as should customer details when it is sold. In the case of a problem, procedures should be in place to be able to trace and possibly recall the product after its supply. (There are fairly regular occurrences of food product recalls, following the discovery of foreign bodies, etc. in items purchased.)

Similarly, in service operations it is frequently necessary to be able to identify the personnel and/or equipment used in the delivery of a service. Although it is not possible to 'batch-mark' an intangible service, effective documentation can be employed to trace relevant details. For example, a vending machine which is filled and cleaned on a regular basis by travelling operator can have a card kept inside, showing the dates the machine was serviced, the batch numbers of ingredients used, and the name of the operator. The card could also show when the supervisor visited and what work was done by the engineer in the case of a breakdown. Such information would be very helpful in pinpointing possible causes in the event of any problems.

The emphasis on traceability should be on 'where appropriate'. Traceability procedures can be very time consuming and expensive to put into practice, especially when product recalls are involved, and should be incorporated only if absolutely necessary.

PAGE 30

AUDIT CHECKLIST

BS EN ISO 9000

4.8 PRODUCT IDENTIFICATION AND TRACEABILITY

	SCORE	COMMENTS
Where appropriate, are there documented procedures to identify the product during:		
pre-processing?	0 1 2 3	
production?	0 1 2 3	
delivery?..	0 1 2 3	
installation?	0 1 2 3	
Where traceability is a specific requirement, are products uniquely identifiable, individually or by batch?...............	0 1 2 3	
Is this identification and associated data recorded?...	0 1 2 3	

MAXIMUM SCORE 18   TOTAL SCORE_____

OUTSTANDING MATTERS   ACTION BY – WHOM   WHEN

AUDIT NO_____ DATE_____ AUDITOR_____ PAGE 30

AUDIT GUIDE

BS EN ISO 9000

4.9 PROCESS CONTROL
(Not applicable to BS EN ISO 9003)

WHAT IS A PROCESS?

Before looking in detail at the requirements for process control, it is appropriate to consider processes and their definition.

Most dictionaries include the word 'manufacture' in their definitions, but one gives it simply and more aptly as 'an activity'. Processes are usually associated with manufacturing industry, for example chemical processes, the printing process, production processes, etc. This part of BS EN ISO 9000 is concerned with processes, but is as applicable to service providers as to manufacturing.

In any activity or process, the state of things at the end is different from that at the beginning. For example, in the process of writing a letter, a blank piece of paper is converted into a meaningful document for someone to read. To produce the letter, the following are necessary:

equipment – pen, table, chair;
materials – paper, envelope, ink, stamps;
information – recipient's address, postal rates;
skills – language and writing skills.

These are shown graphically in Fig. B.3.

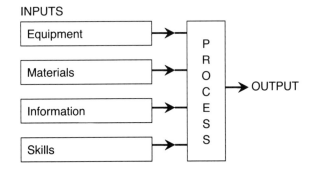

Fig. B.3   Processes

All activities in any organisation consist of a process or combination of processes, each requiring its own inputs to produce output. In order to predetermine and control the output it is necessary to control the inputs. In our example, if the pen is faulty or the ink too thick, the quality of the writing will suffer. If the address is incorrect the letter will not arrive at the desired destination, and if the letter is written in Chinese, the European recipient will not understand it.

A process can describe both manufacturing and service operations on all scales; think of any activity from making a pot of tea to landing an astronaut on Mars: all can be described in these terms.

The output of each process will be part of the input of the next, except at the end of the line when the output will go to the customer. In terms of total quality management, each process

PAGE 31A

is the customer of the previous process and the supplier of the next, and to ensure quality all along the line it is necessary to establish each internal customer's requirements and make the previous process meet them by controlling its inputs. If each internal customer's needs are satisfied the end product will be of the required quality.

The key then in designing a process, having determined the output requirements, is to determine the input requirements and their acceptable tolerances in order to achieve the desired result, and thus control the process by ensuring that the inputs are themselves controlled.

If a process fails to give the required output it is necessary to establish which of the inputs has failed. By pinpointing this exactly it will be possible to take action to correct the input to bring the process back into conformity; this is process control.

In any organisation all the processes must be isolated and the sub-processes separated from the main activities; the output and input requirements for each can then be determined. Take the admission of a hospital patient, for example; this could be broken down into many individual processes, as Fig. B.4 demonstrates. What are the output requirements of each? What are the input requirements in terms of equipment, materials, information and skills, and what criteria must be met for the outputs to satisfy the requirements?

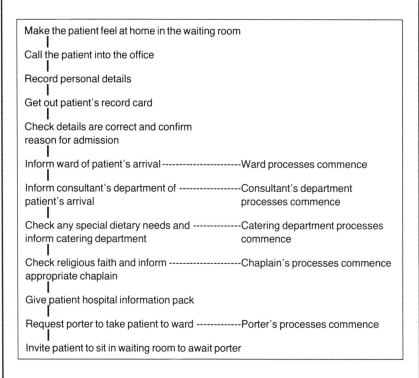

Fig. B.4   The processes of admission of a hospital patient

AUDIT GUIDE

BS EN ISO 9000

4.9 PROCESS CONTROL

GENERAL
(Not applicable to BS EN ISO 9003)

QUALITY SYSTEM REQUIREMENTS

Where appropriate the organisation must identify, plan and control the processes which affect quality in production, installation and servicing. Control includes:

documented procedures for production, installation and servicing where the quality of the process output would be adversely affected in their absence;

provision of suitable equipment and environment;

compliance with reference standards and quality systems;

monitoring and control of suitable process parameters and product characteristics;

use of approved processes and equipment, as appropriate;

clearly defined standards of workmanship, reference samples, etc.;

maintenance of equipment for continued process capability.

NOTES

Having identified the key processes where the product or service needs to be controlled in order to obtain the required quality, it is necessary to plan them in terms of their output and input requirements, and provide detailed documented procedures and work instructions for the successful completion of tasks. Particularly where control is subjective (e.g. for hardness/softness, colour, etc.), reference samples should be provided; these will need to be issues within the document control procedures (see section 4.5, page 22 *et seq.*).

The documented procedures and instructions must identify the skills needed, any setting up requirements, equipment and materials to be used, and any maintenance to be done. Evidence will have to be provided to show that these requirements have been met. Also the capability of the process to produce the required quality must be demonstrable; consideration should be given to how the process is to be monitored and how the output is to be measured to ensure conformance. Here the application of statistics and statistical process control (SPC) are usual (see section 4.20, page 55).

In documenting work instructions, thought must be given to the skills of the personnel who will be using them and the training they will have received. It is not necessary to go into great detail about how a weld is performed if that type of welding is standard practice for the calibre of person performing the operation.

Equipment and environment can contribute greatly to the output of a process. Equipment should be approved as suitable for the process and factors such as lighting and comfort levels considered to enable the process to be effective and efficient.

AUDIT CHECKLIST

BS EN ISO 9000

4.9 PROCESS CONTROL

GENERAL
(Not applicable to BS EN ISO 9003)

	SCORE	COMMENTS
Where quality is directly affected, are the production (and installation if applicable) processes formally:		
identified?..	0 1 2 3	
planned?	0 1 2 3	
Where their absence could affect product quality, are documented procedures and/or drawings available?	0 1 2 3	
Is suitable equipment available?.....................	0 1 2 3	
Is the working environment suitable?..............	0 1 2 3	
Is there the means of compliance with appropriate reference standards/codes and quality plans?...	0 1 2 3	
Are the processes/equipment approved?	0 1 2 3	
Are the process parameters and product characteristics monitored and recorded?........	0 1 2 3	
Are the criteria for workmanship clearly defined, in writing or by drawings and/or samples?	0 1 2 3	
Is the process equipment maintained to suitable standards?..	0 1 2 3	

MAXIMUM SCORE 30   TOTAL SCORE_____

OUTSTANDING MATTERS   ACTION BY – WHOM   WHEN

AUDIT NO_____ DATE_____ AUDITOR_____   PAGE 31

AUDIT GUIDE

BS EN ISO 9000

4.9 PROCESS CONTROL (cont.)

SPECIAL PROCESSES
(Not applicable to BS EN ISO 9003)

QUALITY SYSTEM REQUIREMENTS

Processes, the results of which cannot be fully verified by inspection and testing, and where faults may only become apparent after a period of use of the product, must be subject to continuous monitoring and control of process parameters in line with documented procedures to ensure that the requirements are met.

The equipment and personnel qualifications needed in such processes to achieve the required quality must be defined.

Records must be maintained for such processes, including equipment and personnel involved.

NOTES

This part of section 4.9 refers to what are frequently identified as 'special' or 'qualified' processes. The effectiveness of these cannot be satisfactorily determined by inspection or testing. Take for example the case of the casting of a reinforced concrete bridge component. It will be impossible (without destructive testing) to determine from the finished product various critical factors such as the composition of the concrete mix and its uniformity throughout the component, and the dimensions and spacing of the reinforcing rods. Deficiencies may only come to light if the component fails after the bridge has been in use for a few years.

All the requirements for processes detailed on page 31 apply, but additional controls are vital in such cases. Any equipment or skills necessary to achieve the right quality must be defined and documented. In the production of the concrete component it will be essential for the mixture to be carefully controlled and for there to be a means of verifying that the correct reinforcing rods are used and are correctly spaced during its manufacture. Such verifications must be recorded, along with details of the materials, equipment and personnel employed. Also, a means of tracing the individual component and relating it to the records may be needed (see section 4.8, Product Identification and Traceability, page 30).

Certain industries have standard procedures for special processes.

AUDIT CHECKLIST

BS EN ISO 9000

4.9 PROCESS CONTROL (cont.)

SPECIAL PROCESSES
(Not applicable to BS EN ISO 9003)

	SCORE	COMMENTS
Are any special processes separately identified?	0 1 2 3	
Do they comply with the general requirements (see page 31)?	0 1 2 3	
In addition, are they continuously monitored to ensure that specific requirements are met?....................................	0 1 2 3	
Are the requirements for operators and/or equipment specified?......................................	0 1 2 3	
Are records maintained for special processes relating to:		
equipment used?...	0 1 2 3	
personnel employed?.................................	0 1 2 3	

MAXIMUM SCORE 18   TOTAL SCORE_____

OUTSTANDING MATTERS	ACTION BY – WHOM	WHEN

AUDIT NO_____ DATE_____ AUDITOR_____ PAGE 32

AUDIT GUIDE

BS EN ISO 9000

4.10 INSPECTION AND TESTING

4.10.1 GENERAL

QUALITY SYSTEM REQUIREMENTS

The organisation must establish and maintain documented procedures for inspection and testing to ensure that all the specified requirements of the products or services are met.

The procedures must detail or refer to the inspections and tests to be made and the records to be kept.

NOTES

Detailed notes are given in the following pages:

Receiving Inspection and Testing, section 4.10.2, page 34,
In-process Inspection and Testing, section 4.10.3, page 35,
Final Inspection and Testing, section 4.10.4, page 36,
Inspection and Test Records, section 4.10.5, page 37.

PAGE 33

AUDIT CHECKLIST

BS EN ISO 9000

4.10 INSPECTION AND TESTING

4.10.1 GENERAL

	SCORE	COMMENTS
Are there documented procedures for the inspection and testing activities for:		
incoming product?	0 1 2 3	
process control?	0 1 2 3	
control of finished product?	0 1 2 3	
Are there procedures for the recording of inspection and test results?	0 1 2 3	

MAXIMUM SCORE 12   TOTAL SCORE_____

OUTSTANDING MATTERS   ACTION BY – WHOM   WHEN

AUDIT NO_____ DATE_____ AUDITOR_____   PAGE 33

AUDIT GUIDE

BS EN ISO 9000

4.10 INSPECTION AND TESTING (cont.)

4.10.2 RECEIVING INSPECTION AND TESTING

QUALITY SYSTEM REQUIREMENTS

The organisation must ensure that incoming material is not used or processed (except as below) until it has been inspected and/or tested and its conformance with specified requirements confirmed.

The nature and extent of inspection and testing of incoming material must be determined by the degree of control practised at the supplier's premises and its record of providing conforming material.

Incoming material may be permitted to bypass the receiving inspection process if it is needed urgently, but must be fully documented and traceable in order to allow for recall later if problems arise.

NOTES

Incoming products (raw materials, subcontracted items and services) should be inspected and tested against the specifications and other details quoted or referred to in the purchase order and other purchasing data (see Purchasing, section 4.6, page 25 *et seq.*).

The type of product and the supplier's previous record of providing material of the required standard will determine the level of inspection and testing on receipt of incoming goods; this may be anything from checking labelling on boxes for the correct product and quantity (in the case of cartons of wood-screws, for example), through random sampling of more complex products from a supplier of proven reliability, to 100 per cent inspections of key components which have a major influence on the quality of the finished product. It is up to the organisation to set out the procedures for each product and supplier. The recorded results, i.e. the quantities passing and failing inspections and tests, will help assess whether the levels are correct and can be used to make changes in the inspection rates if necessary.

An example of a flexible procedure could be:

A random sample of 1 per cent of a batch of component XYZ is inspected.
If any defects are found in the 1 per cent sample, a further 10 per cent sample is inspected.
If 1 per cent or more of defects are found in the 10 per cent sample (i.e. one tenth of the sample) the batch is subjected to 100 per cent inspection.
If 2 per cent or more of defects are found in the 10 per cent sample (i.e. one fifth of the sample) the batch is rejected and returned to the supplier.

All non-conforming product must be identified (see Control of Non-conforming Product, section 4.13, page 41 *et seq.*).

PAGE 34

AUDIT CHECKLIST

BS EN ISO 9000

4.10 INSPECTION AND TESTING (cont.)

4.10.2 RECEIVING INSPECTION AND TESTING

	SCORE	COMMENTS
Is incoming product subjected to the verification procedures prior to being released for use or processed?......................	0 1 2 3	
Does the nature and extent of receiving inspection take into account the level of such at the supplier's premises?....................	0 1 2 3	
If any incoming product bypasses the verification process, is it		
positively identified	0 1 2 3	
traceable	0 1 2 3	
in case of subsequent recall due to its possible non-conformance?		
Is non-conforming product identified?	0 1 2 3	

MAXIMUM SCORE 15   TOTAL SCORE_____

OUTSTANDING MATTERS   ACTION BY – WHOM   WHEN

AUDIT NO_____ DATE_____ AUDITOR_____ PAGE 34

AUDIT GUIDE

BS EN ISO 9000

4.10 INSPECTION AND TESTING (cont.)

4.10.3 IN-PROCESS INSPECTION AND TESTING

QUALITY SYSTEM REQUIREMENTS

The organisation must make in-process inspections and tests in accordance with the quality plan and have procedures to ensure that product conforms with the requirements.

Product must be held from further processing until such inspections and tests have been carried out and the product's compliance with requirements verified, except when needed urgently, when it may be released subject to later verification and recall procedures (as with receiving inspection).

NOTES

In-process controls provide more satisfactory and cost-effective methods of ensuring product quality than inspections after the event; the earlier a problem is detected, the sooner the process can be corrected and further non-conformities prevented, avoiding the build-up of costly defective production.

As discussed in Process Control, section 4.9, page 31, process outputs should be continually monitored and their inputs adjusted to make corrections as necessary to secure continued conformance to requirements. Inspections and tests can be used to provide the monitoring and as verification of performance to specification.

As with receiving inspections and testing, a flexible approach should be used when developing in-process inspection and testing procedures to enable the control to be placed at the appropriate places and levels, depending on problems experienced in the past. Consider especially the 'points of no return' in production processes, where, once work has gone through the process, faulty material is not easily or cheaply recoverable. These are points before and at which effective controls are essential.

Statistical process control (SPC) can often be a useful tool; see Statistical Techniques, section 4.20, page 55.

Product may bypass the in-process controls if needed urgently, but as with raw materials and receiving inspection, must be fully documented and traceable in case of recall later.

All non-conforming product must be identified, see Control of Non-conforming Product, section 4.13, page 41 *et seq.*

AUDIT CHECKLIST

BS EN ISO 9000

4.10 INSPECTION AND TESTING (cont.)

4.10.3 IN-PROCESS INSPECTION AND TESTING

	SCORE	COMMENTS

Is further processing withheld until the
specified verifications have been carried out? 0 1 2 3

If further processing is carried out
following failure of the verifications,
is the product

positively identified 0 1 2 3

traceable 0 1 2 3

in case of subsequent recall due to its
possible non-conformance?

Is non-conforming product identified? 0 1 2 3

MAXIMUM SCORE 12   TOTAL SCORE_____

OUTSTANDING MATTERS   ACTION BY – WHOM   WHEN

AUDIT NO_____ DATE_____ AUDITOR_____   PAGE 35

AUDIT GUIDE

BS EN ISO 9000

4.10 INSPECTION AND TESTING (cont.)

4.10.4 FINAL INSPECTION AND TESTING

QUALITY SYSTEM REQUIREMENTS

The procedures for final inspection and testing must ensure that all specified receiving and in-process inspections have been carried out and that the results meet the specified requirements.

Final inspections and tests must be in accordance with the procedures and provide evidence of conformance to specified requirements of the finished product. No product is to be released unless all procedures have been satisfactorily completed and the data recorded and authorised.

NOTES

Final inspection is usually the last occasion on which critical eyes can be cast by the organisation on the product before it is seen by the customer; it is therefore the last opportunity to correct any defects to ensure the supply of a quality product. It is also the one inspection and test function that cannot be bypassed in the event of product being required urgently!

If in-process checks are extensive and adequate controls in place to ensure the product's or service's conformance with the specified requirements, then final inspection may simply be a check to ensure that all the previous inspections and tests have been carried out correctly and their results are satisfactory.

If in-process checks are not adequate to give this assurance, then a more thorough final inspection and testing process is necessary to make sure only products and services in accordance with the specifications are delivered to the customer. This is, however, a less satisfactory situation. Any deficiencies found during final inspection will require a degree of repair or correction, or may result in scrap, resulting in wasted labour and/or material; far better to detect the non-conformities at source and to seek methods for prevention.

Before being delivered to the customer, products should be given 'positive release'. That is, their conformance to specification should be confirmed by an authorised person, and delivery should not be permitted to take place without evidence of that authorisation. Depending on the requirements of the customer and the quality system, this could take the form of certificates of conformity or, more simply, a signature by an authorised person on the inspection records.

All non-conforming product must be identified (see Control of Non-conforming Product, section 4.13, page 41 *et seq.*).

PAGE 36

AUDIT CHECKLIST

BS EN ISO 9000

4.10 INSPECTION AND TESTING (cont.)

4.10.4 FINAL INSPECTION AND TESTING

	SCORE	COMMENTS
Does final inspection ensure that all previous receiving and in-process verifications have been carried out?...............	0 1 2 3	
Is evidence of conformance of the product to specified requirements produced?..............	0 1 2 3	
Is release of the product to the customer withheld until:		
all documented procedures have been satisfactorily completed?............................	0 1 2 3	
all associated documentation is available and authorised?	0 1 2 3	
Is a positive and authorised release of the product made?	0 1 2 3	
Is non-conforming product identified?.............	0 1 2 3	

MAXIMUM SCORE 18   TOTAL SCORE_____

OUTSTANDING MATTERS   ACTION BY – WHOM   WHEN

AUDIT NO_____ DATE_____ AUDITOR_____   PAGE 36

AUDIT GUIDE

BS EN ISO 9000

4.10 INSPECTION AND TESTING (cont.)

4.10.5 INSPECTION AND TEST RECORDS

QUALITY SYSTEM REQUIREMENTS

The organisation must establish and maintain records to provide evidence of the product's performance in inspections and tests related to the acceptance criteria.

The records must identify the authority responsible for the release of product.

NOTES

Records of the product's or service's inspection and test results should be maintained in order to provide a history in case of later deficiencies. It may also be a customer requirement to examine them.

Inspection and test records also provide the organisation with valuable data for an on-going quality improvement programme, e.g. to:

review the adequacy of receiving, in-process and final inspections and tests;

ensure adequacy of process controls;

identify priorities for corrective actions on deficiencies and actions to prevent recurrences of problems (see Corrective and Preventive Actions, section 4.14, page 43 *et seq*.).

provide performance statistics (e.g. 95 per cent of all service calls answered within four hours, 84 per cent of voltmeters exceed their accuracy requirements by 50 per cent, etc.). These statistics are very useful in determining product and servicing developments and providing marketing material.

Inspection and test records form part of the organisation's quality records (see Control of Quality Records, section 4.16, page 51).

AUDIT CHECKLIST

BS EN ISO 9000

4.10 INSPECTION AND TESTING (cont.)

4.10.5 INSPECTION AND TEST RECORDS

	SCORE	COMMENTS
Are records kept giving evidence that the product has met the criteria for acceptance?	0 1 2 3	
Is reference to the defined criteria made in the records?	0 1 2 3	
In the case of a product failing inspection or tests do the records relate to the non-conforming product procedures?	0 1 2 3	
Do the records show the authority responsible for release of product?	0 1 2 3	

MAXIMUM SCORE 12   TOTAL SCORE_____

OUTSTANDING MATTERS   ACTION BY – WHOM   WHEN

AUDIT GUIDE

BS EN ISO 9000

4.11 CONTROL OF INSPECTION, MEASURING AND TEST EQUIPMENT

4.11.1 GENERAL

QUALITY SYSTEM REQUIREMENTS

The organisation must establish and maintain documented procedures to control, maintain and calibrate all measuring and test equipment used to ensure conformance of product to requirements. The measurement certainty of such equipment must be known and it must be used in an appropriate manner consistent with its capabilities.

If required, technical data on test equipment must be available to the customer.

NOTES

All measuring and test equipment used in design, production, inspection, installation and servicing of the product (or service), including hardware (jigs, templates, patterns, etc.) and software, where the quality of the product or service depends on the measurement, must be of suitable calibre for the particular measurements, of known accuracy, and controlled by documented procedures which include the review of the continued suitability of equipment at defined intervals.

Further requirements are detailed in section 4.11.2, page 39.

AUDIT CHECKLIST

BS EN ISO 9000

4.11 CONTROL OF INSPECTION, MEASURING AND TEST EQUIPMENT

4.11.1 GENERAL

	SCORE	COMMENTS
Are there documented procedures to		
control	0 1 2 3	
calibrate	0 1 2 3	
maintain	0 1 2 3	

inspection, measuring and test equipment, including test software?

Is the accuracy of all inspection, measuring and test equipment:

known?	0 1 2 3	
appropriate for the measurements required?	0 1 2 3	

Are test hardware and software, jigs, etc. checked for suitability at prescribed intervals? 0 1 2 3

If required, is technical data on test equipment available for the customer? 0 1 2 3

MAXIMUM SCORE 21   TOTAL SCORE_____

OUTSTANDING MATTERS   ACTION BY – WHOM   WHEN

AUDIT NO_____ DATE_____ AUDITOR_____   PAGE 38

AUDIT GUIDE

BS EN ISO 9000

4.11 CONTROL OF INSPECTION, MEASURING AND TEST EQUIPMENT (cont.)

4.11.2 CONTROL PROCEDURE

QUALITY SYSTEM REQUIREMENTS

The organisation must, within its documented procedures:

determine the measurements to make and select the appropriate equipment capable of making the measurements to the required accuracy;

identify the measuring equipment that can affect product quality and calibrate it against known standards at defined intervals;

define the calibration processes for each piece of equipment, including frequency of checks, methods, accuracy required, acceptance criteria and action to be taken when the results are unsatisfactory;

provide unique identification for each piece of equipment and indicate its calibration status;

in the case of equipment being found to be out of calibration, assess and document the validity of previous inspection results;

maintain records of calibration for all measuring and test equipment;

ensure that the environmental conditions are suitable for the tests and measurements and the calibration of the equipment;

ensure that measuring and test equipment is handled, stored and used in a manner which will preserve its accuracy and fitness for its purpose;

prevent unauthorised adjustment or tampering with measuring and test equipment.

NOTES

Measuring and test equipment must be appropriate for the measurement being made, e.g. if a weight measurement demands an accuracy of $+/-$ 10 grams, the scale used must be capable of measurement to at least that level.

The equipment should be calibrated against known standards, traceable where appropriate to nationally recognised standards, and records kept of calibrations and adjustments needed. The calibrations and methods, frequency of checks, acceptance criteria, etc. should be appropriate for the equipment and its use, and subject to documented procedures. The calibration status of equipment should be immediately apparent, ideally by labelling, showing the date until which that status remains valid.

When measuring and test equipment is found to be out of calibration, there must be procedures to reassess the results of inspections and tests carried out using that equipment since the last satisfactory calibration check. This could result in expensive product recalls, so care needs to be taken regarding the recording of inspection and test results against the equipment used, and in ensuring that, when critical measurements are being made, the equipment is calibrated at the appropriate regular intervals.

Uncalibrated measuring equipment is not to be encouraged; any such should be clearly marked 'Not for use', or similar.

PAGE 39

AUDIT CHECKLIST

BS EN ISO 9000

4.11 CONTROL OF INSPECTION, MEASURING AND TEST EQUIPMENT (cont.)

4.11.2 CONTROL PROCEDURE

	SCORE	COMMENTS
Are the measurements and tests that are to be made in order to determine quality identified, along with tolerances?	0 1 2 3	
Is all equipment used to make quality measurements/tests suitable for each particular application?	0 1 2 3	
Is all such equipment calibrated and adjusted at prescribed intervals, and/or prior to use against certified standards?	0 1 2 3	
Are the calibration processes, methods, frequency and criteria defined?	0 1 2 3	
Are records maintained of the calibration, traceable to the individual piece?	0 1 2 3	
Is the calibration status of each piece of equipment identified?	0 1 2 3	
If equipment is found to be out of calibration, are there procedures to assess the validity of previous test results?	0 1 2 3	
Are the environmental conditions suitable for the measurements, tests and calibrations being made?	0 1 2 3	
Are the storage and use of the inspection, measuring and test equipment suitable for accuracy to be maintained?	0 1 2 3	
Are there procedures to prevent unauthorised adjustment and tampering with such equipment?	0 1 2 3	

MAXIMUM SCORE 30   TOTAL SCORE_____

OUTSTANDING MATTERS   ACTION BY – WHOM   WHEN

AUDIT NO_____ DATE_____ AUDITOR_____ PAGE 39

AUDIT GUIDE

BS EN ISO 9000

4.12 INSPECTION AND TEST STATUS

QUALITY SYSTEM REQUIREMENTS

All material and product in storage, production, installation and servicing must be identifiable as to its conformity or otherwise to the inspections and tests performed. The identification must be by the means determined by the quality plan or documented procedures, to ensure that only conforming material or product is used, despatched or installed.

NOTES

It should be apparent to everyone what any material's or product's inspection or test status is at any time, that is, whether it is awaiting inspection/test, inspected and conforming, or non-conforming. The means of identification should be laid down in the organisation's documented procedures; this is usually achieved by labelling individual products or boxes of product, production or routing cards, or physical location in specifically designated areas. The objective is to ensure that only material or products that have passed inspection and/or tests and conform with the requirements are used for further processing or delivered to the customer.

This requires meticulous care with housekeeping by all personnel. Untidy work areas, jobs left part-done, materials or products unlabelled or placed anywhere other than in the appropriate designated place, etc., all lead to the possibility of confusing good with bad and are to be avoided at all costs.

PAGE 40

AUDIT CHECKLIST

BS EN ISO 9000

4.12 INSPECTION AND TEST STATUS

	SCORE	COMMENTS

Is there a defined method by which the inspection/test status of all product during the

design 0 1 2 3

production 0 1 2 3

inspection/test 0 1 2 3

installation 0 1 2 3

servicing 0 1 2 3

processes is identifiable?

MAXIMUM SCORE 15   TOTAL SCORE_____

OUTSTANDING MATTERS   ACTION BY – WHOM   WHEN

AUDIT NO_____ DATE_____ AUDITOR_____   PAGE 40

AUDIT GUIDE

BS EN ISO 9000

4.13 CONTROL OF NON-CONFORMING PRODUCT

4.13.1 GENERAL

QUALITY SYSTEM REQUIREMENTS

The organisation must establish and maintain documented procedures to ensure that all product not meeting the specified requirements is prevented from being used. This control must include the identification, documentation, evaluation, segregation and disposition of such product, and the notification of all functions concerned.

NOTES

In order that non-conforming product cannot be mistaken for conforming product, any product (that is, raw material, work in progress, or finished product) that does not conform to the specified requirements must be treated as follows.

Identified – the procedures for inspection and test will show which material or product does not conform. It should be immediately and clearly labelled as non-conforming, and the labelling should remain in place until the appropriate action has been taken.

Documented and evaluated – a record of the non-conforming product should be made, indicating:

what the material or product is;
at which stage of processing it is;
the quantity;
the nature and extent of the non-conformity;
who is responsible for its identification as non-conforming;
decisions regarding the product's future disposition.

Segregated – if practical, the non-conforming product should be isolated from conforming material, preferably in a specially designated area, while decisions regarding its disposition are made and effected. In some cases, for example, with a large and difficult-to-move machine, isolation will be impractical. In such cases clear identification of non-conformity is even more important.

PAGE 41

AUDIT CHECKLIST

BS EN ISO 9000

4.13 CONTROL OF NON-CONFORMING PRODUCT

4.13.1 GENERAL

	SCORE	COMMENTS
Are there documented procedures to prevent non-conforming product from being used?......	0 1 2 3	
Is non-conforming product:		
identified?..	0 1 2 3	
isolated (where practical)?	0 1 2 3	
documented?	0 1 2 3	
evaluated?	0 1 2 3	
disposed of by scrap, rework/repair, or use under concession?	0 1 2 3	
Are relevant departments/functions formally notified of non-conforming product?..	0 1 2 3	

MAXIMUM SCORE 21   TOTAL SCORE_____

OUTSTANDING MATTERS   ACTION BY – WHOM   WHEN

AUDIT NO_____ DATE_____ AUDITOR_____   PAGE 41

AUDIT GUIDE

BS EN ISO 9000

4.13 CONTROL OF NON-CONFORMING PRODUCT (cont.)

4.13.2 REVIEW AND DISPOSITION

QUALITY SYSTEM REQUIREMENTS

The responsibility and authority for the review and disposition of non-conforming product must be defined in the organisation's quality system (see Organisation: Responsibility and Authority, section 4.1.2.1, page 2).

Documented procedures must be in place for non-conforming product review, and decisions concerning its disposition.

Where specified in the contract, repaired or reworked product, or that with any other non-conformity, may be supplied only with the agreement of the customer, and the accepted level of repair or non-conformity must be recorded.

Repaired or reworked material must be reinspected and/or retested in accordance with the documented procedures and/or quality plan.

NOTES

When the authorised person reviews non-conforming product, the four most likely outcomes are to reject it/return it to the supplier, scrap it, rework it, or use it under concession.

Repaired or reworked product must undergo inspection and testing in order to ensure its conformity to requirements. Also, it may be necessary to agree with the customer that repaired or reworked product will be supplied, as will certainly be the case for any other non-conforming product. In either case, any agreements and concessions must be subject to the appropriate procedure and formally agreed in writing.

The actions decided regarding non-conforming product disposition, when taken, should be documented along with the original documentation raised when the non-conformity was identified. The results of non-conforming product reviews should be communicated to all functions concerned, and used to help make decisions regarding corrective action and preventive action to avoid future non-conformities (see Corrective and Preventive Action, section 4.14, page 43 *et seq.*). This is an area where most organisations can be pro-active in a quality improvement programme.

PAGE 42

AUDIT CHECKLIST

BS EN ISO 9000

4.13 CONTROL OF NON-CONFORMING PRODUCT (cont.)

4.13.2 REVIEW AND DISPOSITION

	SCORE	COMMENTS
Are the personnel		
responsible for the review...........................	0 1 2 3	
with the authority for the disposition..	0 1 2 3	
of non-conforming product defined?		
Are there documented procedures for the review of non-conforming product?.................	0 1 2 3	
Is repaired or reworked product subject to appropriate reinspection procedures?.........	0 1 2 3	
Are concessions to use repaired and/or substandard product made with the approval of the customer?...............................	0 1 2 3	
In the case of product used under concession, are the details of the non-conformity and the concession recorded?................................	0 1 2 3	

MAXIMUM SCORE 18   TOTAL SCORE_____

OUTSTANDING MATTERS   ACTION BY – WHOM   WHEN

AUDIT NO_____ DATE_____ AUDITOR_____   PAGE 42

AUDIT GUIDE

BS EN ISO 9000

4.14 CORRECTIVE AND PREVENTIVE ACTIONS

4.14.1 GENERAL

QUALITY SYSTEM REQUIREMENTS

The organisation must establish and maintain documented procedures to take corrective and preventive actions on non-conformities.

Corrective and preventive actions on actual or potential non-conformities are to be in proportion to the magnitude of the problems and risks to quality involved.

Any changes to procedures made as the result of such actions must be documented and implemented.

NOTES

Corrective action can be defined as action to correct an existing fault and is usually short-term. For example, an item of product, having been found to be non-conforming, is isolated and dealt with in accordance with the non-conforming product procedures. If that item is to be repaired or reworked, that action can be said to be corrective. Similarly, if a procedure is found to be defective, its development and rewriting would be described as corrective action.

Preventive action is generally more long-term and involves taking and implementing decisions to address the causes of problems to prevent their recurrence. For example, process control on a production line may reveal the regular occurrence of a product defect. The defects themselves are remedied by corrective action, but by analysis of the in-process inspection results a problem is highlighted in the production line which causes the defects. This may perhaps be a piece of faulty machinery or an operator who requires retraining. The repair of the machine or the training of the operator is preventive action, eliminating the cause of the problem and ensuring that it does not keep occurring.

It is in these areas that a quality system can be most effective in improving the efficiency of an organisation. Problems need to be put right by corrective actions, but the analysis of problems and the consequent preventive actions, together with their follow-up and possible changes to procedures, are aimed at developing processes to make permanent improvements.

In implementing corrective and preventive actions it is necessary to set some priorities. Systematic analysis of deficiencies will show which areas need to be targeted for immediate action and which have a lesser urgency. This will depend on the frequency of problems, their ultimate consequences to the product or service, and the resources required to correct and prevent them. Usually the 'Pareto Principle' applies, where 80 per cent of the deficiencies will require 20 per cent of the effort and resources to correct them!

AUDIT CHECKLIST

BS EN ISO 9000

4.14 CORRECTIVE AND PREVENTIVE ACTIONS

4.14.1 GENERAL

	SCORE	COMMENTS
Are there documented procedures to take corrective and preventive action on non-conformities?	0 1 2 3	
Is the degree of corrective and preventive action related to the magnitude of the problem and the risks encountered?	0 1 2 3	
Are changes to procedures implemented and recorded as a result of corrective and preventive actions?	0 1 2 3	

MAXIMUM SCORE 9   TOTAL SCORE_____

OUTSTANDING MATTERS   ACTION BY – WHOM   WHEN

AUDIT NO_____ DATE_____ AUDITOR_____   PAGE 43

AUDIT GUIDE

BS EN ISO 9000

4.14 CORRECTIVE AND PREVENTIVE ACTIONS (cont.)

4.14.2 CORRECTIVE ACTION

QUALITY SYSTEM REQUIREMENTS

The procedures for corrective actions must include:

the effective handling of complaints and reports of non-conformities from customers;

investigating and recording the causes of non-conformities of products, processes and the quality system;

determining the actions necessary to eliminate non-conformities and their causes;

controls to make sure that corrective actions are taken and are effective.

NOTES

Complaining customers are frequently regarded as a nuisance! However, the quality-oriented organisation has a much more enlightened attitude and sees customer complaints more positively as a way of improving the organisation. Customer complaints about a product or service will highlight two important facts: firstly that the product or service is defective and will need corrective action, and secondly that there is a deficiency in the organisation's system which has let a faulty product or service through the inspection and testing procedures – more corrective action required!

Investigating the causes of non-conformities is as important as the corrective action to put them right. This will enable the organisation to implement preventive action which should in turn eliminate the need for that corrective action in the future.

Deciding on the appropriate corrective action is only part of the way to solving the problem; systems must be in place to ensure that the action is taken and that it is effective. It may well be that it is not, and other action has to be taken as a result. Many people are good at making decisions about what to do in order to put something right, but it takes a determined individual to get the problem between his or her teeth and not let it go until it is well and truly dead. Only by closely following up the corrective action to the bitter end can the organisation be sure that the non-conformity has been remedied.

PAGE 44

AUDIT CHECKLIST

BS EN ISO 9000

4.14 CORRECTIVE AND PREVENTIVE ACTIONS (cont.)

4.14.2 CORRECTIVE ACTION

	SCORE	COMMENTS
Are there procedures to:		
handle customer complaints?...................... 0 1 2 3		
investigate the causes of non-conformities? 0 1 2 3		
determine the actions necessary to eliminate causes of non-conformity?........... 0 1 2 3		
Are controls made to ensure that corrective actions are taken and are effective?................ 0 1 2 3		

MAXIMUM SCORE 12   TOTAL SCORE_____

OUTSTANDING MATTERS   ACTION BY – WHOM   WHEN

AUDIT NO_____ DATE_____ AUDITOR_____   PAGE 44

AUDIT GUIDE

BS EN ISO 9000

4.14 CORRECTIVE AND PREVENTIVE ACTIONS (cont.)

4.14.3 PREVENTIVE ACTION

QUALITY SYSTEM REQUIREMENTS

The procedures for preventive action must include:

the use of quality system records to highlight, analyse and eliminate potential causes of non-conformity;

the means to determine actions necessary to prevent non-conformity;

initiation of preventive actions and the application of controls to ensure its effectiveness;

ensuring that relevant information on preventive actions taken is submitted for management review.

NOTES

The entire system of quality records should provide material to highlight the need for preventive action to eliminate potential causes of non-conformity. Such data will come from inspection and test records, internal and external audit reports, non-conforming product reports, service reports, customer complaints, etc. Again, if used positively and interpreted carefully, this wealth of information about defects can indicate where the system is currently breaking down or is likely to do so in the future, and where preventive action is needed. Statistics enthusiasts can have a field day here, and if care is not taken, too many areas of 'possible failure' may come to light. Although each must be considered, it will pay to remember the Pareto Principle and prioritise!

The documented procedures will need to describe the process to deal with problems requiring preventive action, e.g. who is responsible for identifying the problems? What data is used to highlight potential problems and who is responsible for its interpretation? How is priority decided? etc...

As with corrective action, the controls and follow-ups to ensure that preventive action is taken are vital, not only to satisfy the requirements of the Standard, but as part of an organisation's on-going quality improvement programme.

The requirement that preventive actions be submitted for management review (see section 4.1.3, page 5) does not mean that each individual action is to be discussed at the review meetings. A summary of actions and their effectiveness, along with an analysis of how the quality system and quality of product and/or service has changed as a result, will provide the appropriate information.

PAGE 45

AUDIT CHECKLIST

BS EN ISO 9000

4.14 CORRECTIVE AND PREVENTIVE ACTIONS (cont.)

4.14.3 PREVENTIVE ACTION

	SCORE	COMMENTS
Are there procedures to:		
use quality system records to identify and eliminate potential causes of non-conformities?	0 1 2 3	
determine the actions necessary to prevent non-conformity?	0 1 2 3	
Are controls made to ensure that preventive actions are taken and are effective?................	0 1 2 3	
Is information on preventive actions taken submitted for management review?................	0 1 2 3	

MAXIMUM SCORE 12   TOTAL SCORE_____

OUTSTANDING MATTERS   ACTION BY – WHOM   WHEN

AUDIT NO_____ DATE_____ AUDITOR_____   PAGE 45

AUDIT GUIDE

BS EN ISO 9000

4.15 HANDLING, STORAGE, PACKAGING, PRESERVATION AND DELIVERY

4.15.1 GENERAL

QUALITY SYSTEM REQUIREMENTS

The organisation must establish and maintain documented procedures for the handling, storage, packaging, preservation and delivery of the product.

NOTES

This encompasses all materials and products, including raw materials, customer supplied product, work in progress and finished goods, during all stages of processing. Their conformance with requirements must be protected until the organisation's responsibility ends after installation (if applicable) and on delivery or hand-over to the customer.

This is equally applicable to services, which must be completed with evidence that the specified requirements have been met.

Any special requirements for cleaning, packing, moisture proofing, stacking, etc. should be part of the documented procedures.

PAGE 46

AUDIT CHECKLIST

BS EN ISO 9000

4.15 HANDLING, STORAGE, PACKAGING, PRESERVATION AND DELIVERY

4.15.1 GENERAL

	SCORE	COMMENTS
Are there documented procedures for		
handling	0 1 2 3	
storage	0 1 2 3	
packaging..	0 1 2 3	
preservation	0 1 2 3	
delivery...	0 1 2 3	
of the product/service?		

MAXIMUM SCORE 15   TOTAL SCORE_____

OUTSTANDING MATTERS   ACTION BY – WHOM   WHEN

AUDIT NO_____ DATE_____ AUDITOR_____   PAGE 46

AUDIT GUIDE

BS EN ISO 9000

4.15 HANDLING, STORAGE, PACKAGING, PRESERVATION AND DELIVERY (cont.)

4.15.2 HANDLING

QUALITY SYSTEM REQUIREMENTS

The organisation must provide the methods and means of handling products to prevent damage and deterioration.

NOTES

The appropriate means and methods of handling will depend on the product and are likely to include pallets, boxes and containers, conveyor systems, pallet and stacker trucks, etc. They must protect the product from adverse conditions such as shock, vibration, temperature extremes, humidity, corrosion, etc.

The identification of the product must also remain intact.

Instructional documentation, include box labelling, should make reference to any precautions to be taken in handling to ensure the prevention of damage or degradation in quality or performance of the product.

PAGE 47

AUDIT CHECKLIST

BS EN ISO 9000

4.15 HANDLING, STORAGE, PACKAGING, PRESERVATION AND DELIVERY (cont.)

4.15.2 HANDLING

	SCORE	COMMENTS
Does the organisation provide the		
methods	0 1 2 3	
means and resources..................................	0 1 2 3	
of handling the product to prevent damage and deterioration?		
MAXIMUM SCORE 6 TOTAL SCORE_____		

OUTSTANDING MATTERS   ACTION BY – WHOM   WHEN

AUDIT NO_____ DATE_____ AUDITOR_____   PAGE 47

AUDIT GUIDE

BS EN ISO 9000

4.15 HANDLING, STORAGE, PACKAGING, PRESERVATION AND DELIVERY (cont.)

4.15.3 STORAGE

QUALITY SYSTEM REQUIREMENTS

The organisation must provide designated storage facilities for materials and products to prevent damage or deterioration. The means of access to stock for delivery or withdrawal must be specified.

Stock must be reviewed at appropriate intervals to detect deterioration.

NOTES

The storage facilities must be appropriate for the type of stock to prevent damage by corrosion, insects and vermin, dirt, vandalism, etc.

Documented procedures should include the regular inspection of stock for damage and deterioration, and any requirements for stock rotation to allow old stock to be used first.

Damaged or deteriorated stock, and any that has exceeded its shelf-life (or is likely to during further processing) should be treated as non-conforming product and dealt with accordingly (see Control of Non-conforming Product, section 4.13, page 41 *et seq.*).

Only defined personnel should be authorised to have access to stock, which should be kept in an area specifically designated for the purpose. Security should be in accordance with the type of stock and the required limitations of access.

AUDIT CHECKLIST

BS EN ISO 9000

4.15 HANDLING, STORAGE, PACKAGING, PRESERVATION AND DELIVERY (cont.)

4.15.3 STORAGE

	SCORE	COMMENTS
Does the organisation use designated storage for the product to prevent damage and deterioration?	0 1 2 3	
Are there procedures for authorising receipt and issue to and from storage?	0 1 2 3	
Is the condition of stock checked for deterioration at appropriate intervals?.............	0 1 2 3	
If appropriate, is stock rotated to provide for first in, first out?	0 1 2 3	

MAXIMUM SCORE 12   TOTAL SCORE_____

OUTSTANDING MATTERS   ACTION BY – WHOM   WHEN

AUDIT GUIDE

BS EN ISO 9000

4.15 HANDLING, STORAGE, PACKAGING, PRESERVATION AND DELIVERY (cont.)

4.15.4 PACKAGING

QUALITY SYSTEM REQUIREMENTS

The organisation must ensure that packaging, preservation and identification of the product ensures its continued conformance with the requirements from the time of receipt until delivery to the customer.

NOTES

For many products, particularly those needing purpose-made packaging, the packaging will be considered at the design stage; in some cases the packaging will be more complex than the product itself!

The packaging, including the materials used and the labelling or other means of identification, must be appropriate to protect the materials or products whilst under the responsibility of the organisation.

As with handling and storage, the packaging must protect against any hazards likely (within reason) to be encountered. The same product may require different packaging for delivery to different locations; for example, for a delivery of garments to a customer in the same town, a hanging rail on castors with a polythene cover may suffice, but for delivery by sea to the tropics it will require more substantial vermin-proof packaging. Documented procedures must account for the requirements.

Packaging should clearly display reference to the contents, and any specific handling and storage requirements.

PAGE 49

AUDIT CHECKLIST

BS EN ISO 9000

4.15 HANDLING, STORAGE, PACKAGING, PRESERVATION AND DELIVERY (cont.)

4.15.4 PACKAGING

	SCORE	COMMENTS
Does the packaging adequately		
preserve	0 1 2 3	
identify	0 1 2 3	
segregate	0 1 2 3	
the product for such time as is necessary?		

MAXIMUM SCORE 9   TOTAL SCORE_____

OUTSTANDING MATTERS   ACTION BY – WHOM   WHEN

AUDIT GUIDE

BS EN ISO 9000

4.15 HANDLING, STORAGE, PACKAGING, PRESERVATION AND DELIVERY (cont.)

4.15.5 PRESERVATION
4.15.6 DELIVERY

QUALITY SYSTEM REQUIREMENTS

The organisation must arrange for the preservation and segregation of product during the time it is under its control.

Where delivery is contracted, this protection must be maintained following final inspection and testing until delivery to the final destination.

NOTES

Refer to the notes on handling, storage and packaging, pages 46–49, most of which apply during storage following final inspection and delivery.

In the case of a limited shelf-life, this usually commences during manufacture, so care must be taken to ensure that finished stock is delivered in order and that adequate shelf-life remains to meet the requirements of the customer.

AUDIT CHECKLIST

BS EN ISO 9000

4.15 HANDLING, STORAGE, PACKAGING, PRESERVATION AND DELIVERY (cont.)

4.15.5 PRESERVATION
4.15.6 DELIVERY

	SCORE	COMMENTS
Are appropriate measures taken to preserve and segregate the product at all times?...........	0 1 2 3	
Where delivery is a contractual requirement, are there procedures for the protection of the quality of the product during transit to its destination?...	0 1 2 3	

MAXIMUM SCORE 6   TOTAL SCORE_____

OUTSTANDING MATTERS   ACTION BY – WHOM   WHEN

AUDIT GUIDE

BS EN ISO 9000

4.16 CONTROL OF QUALITY RECORDS

QUALITY SYSTEM REQUIREMENTS

In order to demonstrate conformance to the specified requirements and the effective operation of the quality system, the organisation must establish and maintain documented procedures for the identification, collection, indexing, filing, storage and disposition of quality records, including those relating to subcontractors.

Quality records, whether as hard copy or electronic media, must be legible, stored so as to prevent deterioration and loss and be accessible readily as required. Retention times for each document should be agreed and recorded.

Where contractually agreed, quality records must be available for inspection by customers.

NOTES

Quality records are the proof (or otherwise) that a quality system works, and provide a history of its development. (They are a prime target for BS EN ISO 9000 assessors; they will need to see how well the systems have been implemented, and the effects they have had over the course of time.)

The exact nature of quality records will depend on the organisation and its products and services, but they may involve data on computer disk as well as paper, and will certainly include the following:

    Management reviews (section 4.1.3, page 5)
    Quality plans (section 4.2.3, page 8)
    Contract reviews (section 4.3, pages 9–12)
    Design records, if applicable (section 4.4, pages 13–21)
    Document issue/changes records (section 4.5, pages 22–24)
    Purchasing records, if applicable (section 4.6, pages 25–28)
    Traceability data, if applicable (section 4.8, page 30)
    Process records, if applicable (section 4.9, pages 31–32)
    Inspection and testing criteria and results (section 4.10, pages 33–37)
    Calibration records (section 4.11, pages 38–39)
    Non-conforming product data (section 4.13, pages 41–42)
    Records of corrective and preventive actions (section 4.14, pages 43–45)
    Internal quality audits (section 4.17, page 52)
    Training records (section 4.18, page 53)
    Servicing records, if applicable (section 4.19, page 54).

All quality records should be on purpose-made forms and controlled, issued and authorised in the same way as the other quality system documentation (see section 4.5, Document and Data Control, pages 22 *et seq.*). The collection and maintenance of the records must be documented as a procedure; this can be quite a complex operation in an organisation of any size.

A master list of all forms, showing their revision status and the agreed retention period, should be maintained.

PAGE 51

AUDIT CHECKLIST

BS EN ISO 9000

4.16 CONTROL OF QUALITY RECORDS

	SCORE	COMMENTS
Is the effective working of the quality system demonstrable by quality records; are there comprehensive records covering all key aspects of the quality system?	0 1 2 3	

Are there documented procedures for

identification	0 1 2 3	
collection	0 1 2 3	
indexing, filing and storage in a suitable and secure environment, and available for ready retrieval	0 1 2 3	
maintenance and updating	0 1 2 3	
disposition, with established and recorded retention times..............................	0 1 2 3	

of quality records?

Are quality records legible and referenced to the relevant product?	0 1 2 3	
Where contractually agreed, are quality records available for examination by customers?	0 1 2 3	
Where appropriate, are quality records maintained for subcontractor activity?.............	0 1 2 3	

MAXIMUM SCORE 27   TOTAL SCORE_____

OUTSTANDING MATTERS   ACTION BY – WHOM   WHEN

AUDIT NO_____ DATE_____ AUDITOR_____ PAGE 51

AUDIT GUIDE

BS EN ISO 9000

4.17 INTERNAL QUALITY AUDITS

QUALITY SYSTEM REQUIREMENTS

The organisation must establish and maintain documented procedures for a comprehensive system of planned audits of the quality system to verify that all activities comply with the requirements of the system and to measure its effectiveness. Audits must be scheduled on the basis of the status and importance of the activity and be carried out by personnel independent of the activity being audited.

The audits must be documented and the results brought to the attention of those who have responsibility for the functions being audited. The procedures must include the instigation and follow-up of actions found necessary as a result of the audits, which must be the responsibility of the management concerned.

Follow-up action must be audited and its implementation and effectiveness recorded.

NOTES

Refer to section A, chapter 5, of this book for information about conducting quality audits. Also, the international standard ISO 10011 will give guidance.

As with quality records, quality audits establish the effectiveness of the quality system, and provide a basis for development. They too are a target for close scrutiny by BS EN ISO 9000 assessors as they give a history of the working of the quality system.

The purpose of internal quality audits is to ensure that the quality system meets the requirements of the organisation, its procedures are understood and followed, and it is effective in its quality objectives. The essential elements, described in detail earlier in this book, are as follows:

Documented procedures should describe the auditing activity.

Audits should be planned and carried out as planned by staff independent of the activity being audited; priority and frequency of auditing will depend on the importance of each activity.

A report for each audit should be written, giving full details of the findings of the audit, deficiencies found and corrective actions agreed.

The appropriate members of management should be informed of the results of the audit (and receive copies of the reports) and take responsibility for corrective action within agreed timescales.

Follow-up checks of corrective actions should be scheduled and take place, and the effectiveness of the corrective action should be recorded.

The review of the quality system audits should form part of the management review process (see Management Responsibility, Management Review, section 4.1.3, page 5).

PAGE 52

AUDIT CHECKLIST

BS EN ISO 9000

4.17 INTERNAL QUALITY AUDITS

	SCORE	COMMENTS
Are there documented procedures to provide internal audits to verify the working of the quality system and its effectiveness?	0 1 2 3	
Are the audits:		
scheduled in accordance with the importance of the activity?...........................	0 1 2 3	
carried out according to the schedule?	0 1 2 3	
independent of the activity being audited?..	0 1 2 3	
Are there procedures for carrying out follow-up actions?	0 1 2 3	
Are the audits and results documented?	0 1 2 3	
Are deficiencies brought to the attention of the management of the function being audited?..	0 1 2 3	
Is corrective action documented, followed up and verified?	0 1 2 3	

MAXIMUM SCORE 24   TOTAL SCORE_____

OUTSTANDING MATTERS   ACTION BY – WHOM   WHEN

AUDIT NO_____ DATE_____ AUDITOR_____   PAGE 52

AUDIT GUIDE

BS EN ISO 9000

4.18 TRAINING

QUALITY SYSTEM REQUIREMENTS

The organisation must establish and maintain documented procedures for identifying the training needs of all personnel performing duties affecting quality, and ensure the effective provision of the appropriate training.

Tasks requiring specific skills will be identified and suitably qualified personnel assigned to them on the basis of their education, training and experience.

Records of training must be maintained.

NOTES

Training should include quality awareness and the requirements of the quality system as well as specific job training, and should be planned and provided by suitably qualified personnel, whether internally or by external providers. If an external training source is used, it should be assessed for its suitability as with any supplier (see Purchasing, section 4.6, page 25 *et seq.*).

In identifying training needs, consideration must be given to the nature of the tasks to be performed, the previous training, qualifications and experience of the individuals, and their records of performance; training provision must be matched to need. Particular skills required by particular tasks may well be identified in the various quality system procedures, especially those related to process control.

Suitable records must be kept for each staff member, showing the needs which have been identified and the training planned and carried out. Regular review of the records should take place so that training can be updated and deficiencies remedied. Many organisations incorporate this into staff appraisal schemes, but review should be more frequent than the once yearly offered by the usual appraisal system. Continual monitoring of training activity is essential to measure its effectiveness.

Training, both in quality- and job-related matters, brings knowledge, skills and abilities to an organisation's human resource to enable its objectives to be met. Time or money spent in the provision of relevant and effective training is seldom wasted.

PAGE 53

AUDIT CHECKLIST

BS EN ISO 9000

4.18 TRAINING

	SCORE	COMMENTS
Are there documented procedures for:		

identifying operations and tasks for
which training is necessary?....................... 0 1 2 3

identifying individual training needs?........... 0 1 2 3

Are training programmes

planned 0 1 2 3

executed 0 1 2 3

in accordance with the above needs?

Is general quality awareness training
carried out:

for new employees as part of
induction?... 0 1 2 3

on an on-going basis for all staff? 0 1 2 3

Is training carried out by qualified
personnel?.. 0 1 2 3

Are records kept of training and
achievement? 0 1 2 3

MAXIMUM SCORE 24   TOTAL SCORE_____

OUTSTANDING MATTERS   ACTION BY – WHOM   WHEN

AUDIT NO_____ DATE_____ AUDITOR_____   PAGE 53

AUDIT GUIDE

BS EN ISO 9000

4.19 SERVICING
(Not applicable to BS EN ISO 9003)

QUALITY SYSTEM REQUIREMENTS

Where servicing is a contractual requirement, the organisation must establish and maintain documented procedures for performing the servicing and verifying so that it meets the specified requirements.

NOTES

Servicing here generally refers to the after-sales servicing and maintenance carried out on a manufactured product, not the provision of services as products like insurance broking, catering, etc. The latter are, in effect, production processes, and their delivery should be governed by the requirements of process control (section 4.9, page 31A *et seq.*).

For after-sales service, there must be procedures to ensure that the provision meets specific requirements. All of the requirements of the rest of the Standard still apply, for example the provision of suitable equipment, inspection and testing, calibrated measuring and test equipment, work instructions where necessary, training, etc. As with any product, servicing (whether after-sales servicing or the provision of a pure service) needs to be carefully designed, produced and tested to meet the needs of the customer.

Standards must also be set for the back-up of the servicing, including technical advice, spare parts availability, response times, etc., and there must be procedures to verify that requirements in the performance of the service and its back-up are being conformed to.

PAGE 54

AUDIT CHECKLIST

BS EN ISO 9000

4.19 SERVICING
(Not applicable to BS EN ISO 9003)

	SCORE	COMMENTS
Where after-sales service is contracted,		
Are there documented procedures for the provision of the servicing?	0 1 2 3	
Are special tools and equipment verified as to their suitability?	0 1 2 3	
Is measuring and test equipment controlled and calibrated as for internal equipment?	0 1 2 3	
Are suitable instructions provided for installation, commissioning and maintenance?	0 1 2 3	
Is there adequate back-up for:		
competent servicing?	0 1 2 3	
technical advice?	0 1 2 3	
spare parts supply?	0 1 2 3	
Is the appropriate training provided for servicing personnel?	0 1 2 3	

MAXIMUM SCORE 24   TOTAL SCORE_____

OUTSTANDING MATTERS   ACTION BY – WHOM   WHEN

AUDIT NO_____ DATE_____ AUDITOR_____ PAGE 54

AUDIT GUIDE

BS EN ISO 9000

4.20 STATISTICAL TECHNIQUES

4.20.1 IDENTIFICATION OF NEED
4.20.2 PROCEDURES

QUALITY SYSTEM REQUIREMENTS

(4.20.1 IDENTIFICATION OF NEED)
The organisation must identify the need for statistical techniques to establish, control and verify process capability and product characteristics.

(4.20.2 PROCEDURES)
The organisation must establish and maintain documented procedures to implement and control the application of statistical techniques identified in 4.20.1.

NOTES

Statistical techniques can be very useful in determining the acceptability of a product or process. Generally restricted to mass production environments, they include sampling techniques, where the acceptability of a batch is determined by the acceptability of a small representative sample, and statistical process controls, where adjustments are made to processes to maintain control when outputs show signs of deviation from requirements.

Statistics, if used correctly, can bring about significant reductions in scrap rates, rework costs and complaints. They can also ensure the reliability of raw materials, and be used as a tool for fault-finding and problem solving.

Section 4.20.1 requires the organisation to identify the need for statistical techniques; if the need is not there, there is no requirement to proceed down this avenue further. If the particular processes employed lend themselves to the use of statistical techniques to establish and control process capability, there are many approaches and techniques available; the first stage is likely to involve process capability studies and organisations without the relevant knowledge will need to seek guidance.

As we are now beginning to go beyond the scope of this book, suffice it to say at this stage that it is vital that the appropriate techniques for the products and processes involved are selected in order to obtain reliable results. Standard techniques should be used where available, otherwise any techniques employed should be proved to be suitable, based on valid statistical theory, and their implementation covered by documented procedures.

AUDIT CHECKLIST

BS EN ISO 9000

4.20 STATISTICAL TECHNIQUES

4.20.1 IDENTIFICATION OF NEED
4.20.2 PROCEDURES

	SCORE	COMMENTS
Are the needs identified for statistical techniques to:		
establish and maintain process capability?..	0 1 2 3	
control process parameters?........................	0 1 2 3	
Are there documented procedures to		
implement	0 1 2 3	
control the application of..............................	0 1 2 3	

the statistical techniques for which
the need has been identified?

MAXIMUM SCORE 12   TOTAL SCORE_____

OUTSTANDING MATTERS   ACTION BY – WHOM   WHEN

AUDIT NO_____ DATE_____ AUDITOR_____   PAGE 55

SECTION C

7

EXAMPLES OF QUALITY SYSTEM DOCUMENTATION

INTRODUCTION

Documentation is a vital part of any quality system. From it we can determine an organisation's quality policy and how it goes about putting that policy into practice, and obtain evidence that the policy and procedures have been implemented and are working effectively.

Because of the nature of BS EN ISO 9000 and its requirements, quality system documentation for organisations seeking or having gained accreditation tends to follow fairly consistent patterns and formats. There are always a quality manual, procedures manual(s) with probable work instructions, and a quantity of other documentation, particularly forms for keeping records. This section of the book gives some examples of typical documentation that an imaginary firm (Atmostat Controls Ltd, manufacturers and suppliers of temperature and humidity control equipment) might use in its quality system as it seeks registration to BS EN ISO 9001. These examples are not a complete quality system, but will give an indication of the format and style of suitable documentation, including all-important references that will tie the whole system together. As well as a complete quality manual, the examples include one full and one part procedures manual, some work instructions, and various other specimens.

Some important things to remember about documentation are:

- it needs to be only as complex as is required by the organisation; avoid the temptation to over-document and provide pieces of paper that are not necessary to control the quality functions;

- it must accurately reflect the actual policies and procedures in use in the organisation; documentation is drawn up after the systems have been devised and proven – it is no use writing the perfect quality manual and set of procedural instructions, and then tailoring the organisation to fit; it just won't work;
- the staff in your organisation are the best people to devise the appropriate procedures (given some guidance as necessary), and then draft the documentation of them, because they are at the 'sharp-end'. After all, presumably your organisation has been run effectively by these people for some time or it would not exist today!

For these reasons it is not a proposition to buy a quality system 'off the shelf'; do not be persuaded otherwise. Similarly, it would be unwise to attempt to copy someone else's documentation – including the examples in this book, though, hopefully they will be a source of assistance for your own inspiration and creativity. Use examples such as these as models only for a system created specifically to meet your needs; you will then be able to devise and implement a quality system that is truly in the ownership of the people in your organisation – what greater incentive for it to be cherished and developed?

So, having learned about quality and quality systems, and the process of planning and seeking accreditation to BS EN ISO 9000, and investigated thoroughly the current standing of your organisation relative to the Standards, your work now begins in earnest. Good luck!

SAMPLE DOCUMENTS

The format of the list of documents in Fig. C.1 is itself an example of a piece of quality documentation, i.e. a master list that might be maintained by the quality manager.

An example of the need to reissue a document following revision is provided by our sample quality manual. Imagine that the manual was first issued in July 1993 without sections on Inspection and Testing, and Control of Non-conforming Product. When these sections were inserted as sections 17 and 20 in January 1994 (note the issue dates in the respective sections), it would have been considered necessary to renumber all the subsequent sections and reissue the entire manual as Issue 2. Then, following the revision of BS 5750/ISO 9000 in 1994 to BS EN ISO 9000, it was necessary to make various changes to Atmostat Control Ltd's quality system to bring it into line, hence Issue 3. (Note that the nature of these latter changes is indicated where they occur.)

In the case of our sample procedures documents, PROC-07 AND PROC-05, only minor revisions have taken place (as indicated on page 1 in each case) since they were first issued. It was not considered necessary to reissue the entire documents on this occasion, only the amended pages.

ATMOSTAT CONTROLS LTD
MASTER LIST OF QUALITY DOCUMENTS

	Ref.	Title	Issue	Date
1	QM-01	Quality Manual	3	Feb. 95
2	PROC-07	Control of Non-conforming Product	1	Dec. 93
3	NCPL-01	Non-conforming Product Label	1	Nov. 93
4	SCRL-01	Scrap Label	1	Nov. 93
5	NCR-01	Non-conformity Report	1	Dec. 93
6	WI-07-01	Work Instruction	2	Dec. 93
7	WAN-01	Weekly Analysis of Non-conformities	1	Dec. 93
8	PROC-05	Inspection and Testing	1	Jan. 94
9	ITP-3009	Inspection/Test Procedure	1	Dec. 93
10	ITP-5112	Inspection/Test Procedure	1	Dec. 93
11	RIREP-01	Receiving Inspection Report	1	Sep. 93
12	CREV-01	Contract Review Record	1	Dec. 93
13	CALIB-01	Calibration Record	1	Jan. 93
14	DTRP-01	Department Training Plan	2	Oct. 92
15	TRREC-01	Training Record	2	Oct. 92
16	SCL-01	Service Call Log	3	Sep. 93
17	CCFM-01	Customer Complaint	1	Aug. 93
18	SAQ-01	Supplier Assessment Questionnaire	1	Aug. 93

Also included as examples of quality records:
19   Job description – service manager
20   Minutes of quarterly management quality review meeting
21   Internal audit report

Ref: LIST-01   Issue: 3 Mar. 1995   Page: 1 of 1

Fig. C.1   Master list of quality documents

ATMOSTAT CONTROLS LTD
QUALITY MANUAL

THIS IS A CONTROLLED DOCUMENT AND NOT TO BE COPIED WITHOUT AUTHORISATION FROM THE QUALITY MANAGER. ONLY ORIGINALS, SIGNED BY THE MANAGING DIRECTOR, MAY BE USED AS WORKING DOCUMENTS.

MANUAL NO: 01

CONTENTS

	Section	Page	Clause*	Issue
Authorised Holders	1	2		1
Control of the Manual	2	3		1
Introduction	3	4		1
Company Quality Policy	4	5	4.1.1	2
Organisation	5	6	4.1.2.1	1
Resources	6	7	4.1.2.2	2
Management Representative	7	8	4.1.2.3	1
Management Review	8	9	4.1.3	2
Quality System	9	10	4.2	2
Contract Review	10	12	4.3	1
Design Control	11	13	4.4	1
Document and Data Control	12	14	4.5	2
Purchasing	13	16	4.6	2
Control of Customer Supplied Product	16	17	4.7	2
Product Identification and Traceability	15	17	4.8	1
Process Control	16	18	4.9	1
Inspection and Testing	17	19	4.10	1
Measuring and Test Equipment	18	20	4.11	1
Inspection and Test Status	19	20	4.12	1
Control of Non-Conforming Product	20	21	4.13	1
Corrective and Preventive Action	21	22	4.14	2
Handling, Storage, Packaging and Delivery	22	23	4.15	1
Quality Records	23	24	4.16	1
Internal Quality Auditing	24	25	4.17	1
Employee Training	25	26	4.18	1
Servicing	26	27	4.19	1
Statistical Techniques	27	27	4.20	1

* Refers to relevant clauses of BS EN ISO 9001, 1994

Changes from Issue 2: Complete review and revisions as indicated in the light of changes to ISO 9000, 1994.

This quality manual has been approved by:————————————————

Date:——————

| Ref: QM-01 | Issue: 3 Feb. 1995 | Page: 1 of 27 |

ATMOSTAT CONTROLS LTD
QUALITY MANUAL

1. AUTHORISED HOLDERS (Issue 1, July 1993)

MANUAL NO.:   AUTHORISED HOLDER
    01   Quality manager
    02   Managing director
    03   Technical director
    04   Production director
    05   Commercial director

ATMOSTAT CONTROLS LTD
QUALITY MANUAL

2. CONTROL OF THE MANUAL (Issue 1, July 1993)

Distribution of this manual is the responsibility of the quality manager.

Maintenance of the manual is the responsibility of each registered holder. Revisions are issued as necessary by the quality manager to the registered holders, who are responsible for including the revised pages in their respective manuals, and returning those rendered obsolete to the quality manager.

When revisions are implemented, the revision number of the complete affected section is updated and the section reissued. The amendments are indicated by a vertical line in the left-hand margin and summarised at the end of the section. The revision update is also recorded on the contents page which is reissued with the amendment.

Each time the contents page is revised, the managing director signs the page as an indication of the company's approval of the revised information.

ATMOSTAT CONTROLS LTD
QUALITY MANUAL

3. INTRODUCTION (Issue 1, July 1993)

This quality manual describes the organisation, responsibilities for and procedures used in the control of product quality by Atmostat Controls Ltd.

Its purpose is to enable company personnel to understand the basic techniques and procedures required to maintain the correct quality standards. This quality level is necessary to ensure that the company's products conform to customer specifications.

It is the responsibility of *all* employees to assist in making the procedures in this quality manual effective.

Any procedure in this manual may be amended when necessary and procedures will be reviewed and adjusted as required.

The procedures described in this manual, and the associated procedures manuals and work instructions constitute mandatory practice for all staff.

ATMOSTAT CONTROLS LTD
QUALITY MANUAL

4. COMPANY QUALITY POLICY (Issue 2, Feb. 1993)

Atmostat Controls Ltd will design, supply and maintain environmental control equipment in accordance with its published specifications and the agreed requirements of its customers.

The quality and reliability of the company's products are the concern of every person in the organisation. The company believes that excellence in quality is achieved by creating quality awareness in all employees, and to that end will educate and train its employees in all the required aspects of quality control.

As a manufacturer of quality products, the company will ensure that its policy of continuous quality improvement is maintained. The quality department will review the quality system periodically with other departments to reaffirm its adequacy and conformity to the current requirements of the company and its customers.

In order to achieve its quality objectives, Atmostat Controls Ltd maintains an effective quality system conforming to the requirements of BS EN ISO 9001, 1994.

Signed by:_____ Chairman and managing director

Date:_____ ATMOSTAT CONTROLS LTD

Changes in issue 2: Reference to BS 5750, part 1, 1987 changed to BS EN ISO 9001, 1994.

| Ref: QM-01 | Issue: 3 Feb. 1995 | Page: 5 of 27 |

ATMOSTAT CONTROLS LTD
QUALITY MANUAL

5. ORGANISATION (Issue 1, July 1993)

The organisation chart shows the personnel having direct responsibility for the control and maintenance of the quality system.

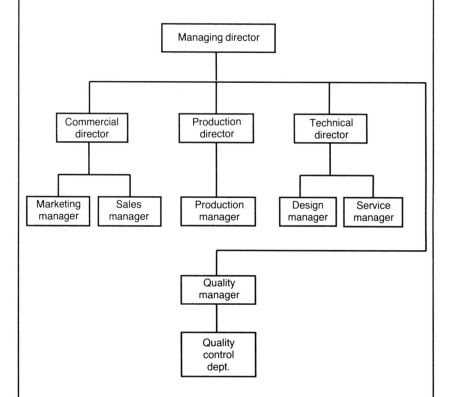

A job description is issued to all personnel, showing each employee's functional and quality-related responsibilities, with master copies filed in the personnel department.

Ref: QM-01 | Issue: 3 Feb. 1995 | Page: 6 of 27

ATMOSTAT CONTROLS LTD
QUALITY MANUAL

6. RESOURCES (Issue 2, Sept. 1994)

The company provides adequate resources by way of trained personnel and equipment to ensure that its products are provided in accordance with its objectives for quality. This includes the company management, inspection and testing of the design, production, installation and servicing of the products, and the continued audit and review of the quality system to ensure its continued suitability and effectiveness.

The adequacy of resources is reviewed in the course of the regular management reviews (ref. section 8).

Changes in Issue 2: Title changed and 'company management' added, in line with 1994 Standard revisions.

| Ref: QM-01 | Issue: 3 Feb. 1995 | Page: 7 of 27 |

ATMOSTAT CONTROLS LTD
QUALITY MANUAL

7. MANAGEMENT REPRESENTATIVE (Issue 1, July 1993)

As the management representative for all matters related to quality, it is the quality manager's overall responsibility to make sure that all departments' activities are in accordance with this quality manual and the associated procedures. This responsibility does not conflict with any other function of the quality manager.

The quality manager is also responsible for the quality control department, whose duties include:

- Supplier and customer liaison involving all matters related to quality.
- Ensuring that raw materials conform to specification and rejecting through the supplier any material found to be defective.
- Ensuring that in-process checks are carried out as specified.
- Ensuring that finished products are inspected/tested according to procedures.
- Updating specifications and establishing current and future test methods.
- Internal calibration of measuring and test equipment.
- Maintaining the quality system and all documentation and records relating to quality.

ATMOSTAT CONTROLS LTD
QUALITY MANUAL

8. MANAGEMENT REVIEW (Issue 2, Oct. 1994)

A management committee, consisting of managers from all key areas of the organisation, meets regularly to review the effectiveness of the quality system.

These meetings are chaired by the quality manager, and the minutes and action points recorded.

Matters reviewed include:

- company quality system,
- verification resources,
- supplier performance,
- in-house defect rates and trends,
- external quality audits,
- internal quality audits,
- training requirements,
- customer complaints,
- corrective and preventive actions,
- quality plans.

Changes in Issue 2: 'and preventive' added to corrective actions, and quality plans added, in line with 1994 Standard revisions.

| Ref: QM-01 | Issue: 3 Feb. 1995 | Page: 9 of 27 |

ATMOSTAT CONTROLS LTD
QUALITY MANUAL

|9. QUALITY SYSTEM (Issue 2, Nov. 1994)

9.1 QUALITY DOCUMENTATION

The company's quality system is recorded and documented in the quality manual.

The quality manual describes the organisation, responsibilities for and procedures used in the control of product quality.

The procedures manuals relate directly to the quality manual and are as follows:

PROC-01   Contract Review
PROC-02   Design Control
PROC-03   Purchasing
PROC-04   Production Procedures
PROC-05   Inspection and Testing
PROC-06   Equipment Calibration
PROC-07   Control of Non-conforming Product
PROC-08   Warehousing and Distribution Procedures
PROC-09   Internal Quality Audits
PROC-10   After-sales Servicing

The procedures manuals refer to work instructions relating to individual operations.

Other documentation essential to the quality system is itemised on a master list held by the quality manager.

All departmental documents shall be reviewed and updated as and when necessary by the departmental heads concerned, in collaboration with the quality department.

Documentation is included in the periodic internal auditing procedures to ensure that the standards required are being implemented and maintained.

Documentation concerning product quality shall be available for inspection on site by customers' representatives during quality system audits. An exception to this rule may be made if information is classified as confidential.

| Ref: QM-01 | Issue: 3 Feb. 1995 | Page: 10 of 27 |

ATMOSTAT CONTROLS LTD
QUALITY MANUAL

9. QUALITY SYSTEM (cont.)

9.2 QUALITY PLANNING

The quality manager is responsible for the planning of all activities related to quality, and for the development, implementation and revision of all quality procedures.

Each of the company's products (or group of products, as appropriate) has a documented quality plan, produced by the technical department and reviewed periodically by management.

Each quality plan describes:

- – the controls, processes, equipment (including inspection and test equipment), resources and skills necessary to achieve the required quality;

- – the compatibility of the design, production processes, inspection and test, installation and servicing procedures;

- – the critical factors (e.g. measurements) related to quality, their tolerances and how they are to be verified;

- – the key elements of fitness for purpose and how they are to be assessed;

- – the documentation and quality records needed for all stages of design, production, inspection and testing, installation and servicing.

Changes in Issue 2: Title changed from 'Quality documentation' to 'Quality system', and section 9.2 'Quality plans' added in line with 1994 Standard revisions.

ATMOSTAT CONTROLS LTD
QUALITY MANUAL

10. CONTRACT REVIEW (Issue 1, July 1993)

10.1 GENERAL

All purchase enquiries are carefully scrutinised to make sure that they conform to the company's product range and production capabilities in accordance with PROC-01, Contract Review.

Technical, production and quality personnel are involved as required in order to establish the customer's precise requirements.

Design requirements and specifications are agreed with the customer. These, along with any details concerning non-conformance, are recorded.

10.2 NEW CONTRACTS

New orders are reviewed to ensure that they agree with the tender and, if so, are passed to design or production as appropriate. Conformity to customer's requirements is confirmed through sampling if required.

10.3 REPEAT CONTRACTS

All repeat orders are reviewed to ensure that the customer's requirements have not been altered from previously agreed levels. Any cases involving a deviation are referred to design and/or production departments as appropriate before commencing production.

Specification changes are in accordance with PROC-02, Design Control.

ATMOSTAT CONTROLS LTD
QUALITY MANUAL

11. DESIGN CONTROL (Issue 1, July 1993)

11.1 GENERAL

Design control is in accordance with the procedures in PROC-02, Design Control.

The design function is structured to ensure that all customer requirements are translated into a specification fully defining the product. When compiling the specification, full consideration is given to the product's producibility and controllability using the proposed methods of manufacture.

It is the responsibility of the technical director to ensure that design procedures are adhered to.

11.2 DESIGN PROCEDURES

PROC-02, Design Control, specifies the design code of practice and includes the following:

- responsibility and authority for design,
- procedures for monitoring the design,
- timing,
- design review/deviation/change control procedures,
- verification,
- compliance with statutory regulations,
- maintenance of records.

11.3 DESIGN SPECIFICATION

The company's design specification systems ensure that all the customer's requirements are met and contain all the information necessary to create the design.

Any deviations are agreed with the customer and recorded.

11.4 DESIGN VERIFICATION

Designs are reviewed throughout the design process in accordance with the review process described in PROC-02, Design Control.

ATMOSTAT CONTROLS LTD
QUALITY MANUAL

12. DOCUMENT AND DATA CONTROL (Issue 2, Jan. 1995)

All references in this section to documents and documentation refer equally to data in hard copy and computer disk forms.

12.1 DOCUMENTATION

The quality manual describes the company's quality policy.

The procedures manuals relate directly to the quality manual and describe the procedural quality-related activities. They detail the methods employed and specifications used to ensure that the finished product meets the customer's requirements.

Documentation essential to the functioning of the quality system is supplied to those areas which require the information on a need-to-know basis.

All quality documentation is itemised on the master list in the keeping of the quality manager. The list includes the revision status.

12.2 ISSUE AND REVISION

Amendments to the company's quality documentation are carried out by the quality control department. All amendments carry an issue number and date. A record is kept of all changes.

The quality control department also ensures that the customer supplied quality documentation and reference material are kept up-to-date.

It is the responsibility of the recipients of amended documentation to ensure that the changes replace existing documents and that the obsolete documents are removed and returned to the quality manager for disposal.

12.3 DOCUMENT CHANGE REQUESTS

Proposals for document changes may be raised by anyone in the company who requires a modification to be considered. These are directed to the quality manager, who will discuss the proposed changes with the departments concerned.

| Ref: QM-01 | Issue: 3 Feb. 1995 | Page: 14 of 27 |

ATMOSTAT CONTROLS LTD
QUALITY MANUAL

12. DOCUMENT AND DATA CONTROL (cont.)

12.4 DOCUMENT DISTRIBUTION

The quality control department maintains a record of the distribution of all copies of procedures, specifications, work instructions, etc.

12.5 FILE MAINTENANCE

Managers and supervisors of all departments concerned have the responsibility to ensure that all documentation required by their department is maintained in an up-to-date and satisfactory condition. They must also ensure that documented procedures and work instructions reflect actual working practices and vice versa.

All relevant information must be readily available to employees as required.

Changes in Issue 2: Title changed and reference to data and computer disks added.

ATMOSTAT CONTROLS LTD
QUALITY MANUAL

13. PURCHASING (Issue 2, Oct. 1994)

13.1 PURCHASE CONTROL

Purchase control is carried out in accordance with PROC-03, Purchasing.

Where not provided by the supplier, Raw material specifications fully detailing all relevant criteria (RMSPEC-01, etc.) provide the basis for the purchase of all material used.

No deviation from the procedures or the specifications is permitted without written approval from the quality manager.

13.2 APPROVED SUPPLIERS

Except with the authority of the quality manager, no materials may be purchased from a supplier not on the list of approved suppliers.

Suppliers are required to submit samples for evaluation and sign the supplier's agreement of conformance before they can be included on the list of approved suppliers. All suppliers are asked to provide full product specifications and health and safety data which are retained on file in the purchasing department.

Close contact is maintained with all key suppliers so that advantage may be taken of any new product developments and that the company is informed of any specification changes.

Regular quality audits are carried out on suppliers. A major consideration in supplier approval is the supplier's own quality system; it is the company's policy to select suppliers approved to BS EN ISO 9000 where possible.

Suppliers are required to provide evidence of conformance to specifications with deliveries.

13.3 PURCHASE RECORDS

Records covering all materials purchased are retained in accordance with PROC-03, Purchasing.

Ref: QM-01   Issue: 3 Feb. 1995   Page: 16 of 27

ATMOSTAT CONTROLS LTD
QUALITY MANUAL

13. PURCHASING (cont.)

13.4 INSPECTION

Incoming raw materials are subject to the inspection procedures in accordance with PROC-05.

13.5 DEFECTIVE PURCHASED RAW MATERIALS

If inspection of raw material indicates that the quality does not meet the specification, then the material is treated as non-conforming material and dealt with in accordance with section 20 of this manual, Control of Non-conforming Product.

Changes in Issue 2: Reference to BS 5750/ISO 9000 changed to BS EN ISO 9000.

14. CONTROL OF CUSTOMER SUPPLIED PRODUCT
(Issue 2, Oct. 1994)

The control of customer supplied products is described in PROC-03, Purchasing. The quality control department carries out inspections and tests as specified, and any deficiencies are reported to the customer and relevant departments.

Any material not meeting the requirements is dealt with in accordance with section 20 of this manual, Control of Non-conforming Product.

Changes in Issue 2: Title changed in line with 1994 Standard revisions.

15. PRODUCT IDENTIFICATION AND TRACEABILITY
(Issue 1, July 1993)

All products are labelled or batch-marked as specified in the procedures manuals.

The use of labelling and batch marking ensures full product identification and traceability.

| Ref: QM-01 | Issue: 3 Feb. 1995 | Page: 17 of 27 |

ATMOSTAT CONTROLS LTD
QUALITY MANUAL

16. PROCESS CONTROL (Issue 1, July 1993)

Customer orders are passed from the sales department to the production department on internal order forms, ref. IO-01.

All products are fully specified in terms of raw materials and characteristics in the relevant technical files.

All raw materials are checked against the appropriate specifications by the quality control department before being used in production (ref. section 17, Inspection and Testing).

16.1 PROCESS INSTRUCTIONS

Written procedures and work instructions covering each stage of the manufacturing process are fully detailed in PROC-04, Production procedures.

These instructions cover the following:

- clearly defined stages of the manufacturing processes,
- sequence of operations,
- precautions in handling,
- specific customer requirements,
- references to process control testing,
- record keeping,
- product, traceability and quality status identification,
- storage and packaging.

The criteria for workmanship are clearly stipulated for each manufacturing step, illustrated by the use of work instructions, drawings, master samples and technical files where applicable.

It is the responsibility of the production manager and his or her supervisors to ensure that the correct procedures are adhered to and that the necessary records are kept.

ATMOSTAT CONTROLS LTD
QUALITY MANUAL

17. INSPECTION AND TESTING (Issue 1, Jan. 1994)

Inspection and testing are carried out in accordance with PROC-05, Inspection and Test Procedures.

17.1 RECEIVING INSPECTION AND TESTING

All raw materials and components received by the company for use in its products are controlled to defined standards by inspection and testing in accordance with procedure manual PROC-05, section 2.

Only raw materials which are correct to specification, or have a permissible deviation, will be placed in stock for production use.

Substandard or non-conforming materials are identified and dealt with in accordance with section 20 of this manual, Control of Non-conforming Product, and the supplier is notified accordingly.

17.2 IN-PROCESS INSPECTION AND TESTING

Production operatives and the quality control department carry out control checks in accordance with procedure manual PROC-05, section 3.

Substandard or non-conforming materials and/or work are identified and dealt with in accordance with section 20 of this manual, Control of Non-conforming Product.

17.3 FINAL INSPECTION AND TESTING

Each production order of finished goods is inspected and tested in accordance with procedure manual PROC-05, section 4.

Samples are retained where applicable.

Substandard or non-conforming materials and/or work are identified and dealt with in accordance with section 20 of this manual, Control of Non-conforming Product.

ATMOSTAT CONTROLS LTD
QUALITY MANUAL

18. MEASURING AND TEST EQUIPMENT (Issue 1, July 1993)

All measuring and test equipment used in the production processes, and that used for inspection and testing, is subject to periodic calibration to the relevant standards as laid down in PROC-06, Equipment Calibration. These procedures include:

- traceability of equipment to calibration records,
- calibration status of equipment,
- calibration procedures and standards,
- calibration frequency,
- procedures in the event of calibration failure,
- handling and storage of test equipment,
- reference standards,
- record maintenance.

19. INSPECTION AND TEST STATUS (Issue 1, July 1993)

The inspection and test status of all materials at all stages of processing is identified using the systems laid down in the procedure manuals PROC-03, Purchasing, PROC-04, Production Procedures and PROC-05, Inspection and Test Procedures.

Material not conforming to the relevant specifications is isolated and dealt with in accordance with section 20 of this manual, Control of Non-conforming Product.

The final release of material in the areas for non-conforming product is carried out by the quality manager or his/her deputy.

| Ref: QM-01 | Issue: 3 Feb. 1995 | Page: 20 of 27 |

ATMOSTAT CONTROLS LTD
QUALITY MANUAL

20. CONTROL OF NON-CONFORMING PRODUCT
(Issue 1, Jan. 1994)

Inspection and testing procedures are described in PROC-05, Inspection and Test Procedures.

In the event of a failure to achieve the approved standard, the procedures detailed in PROC-07, Control of Non-conforming Product, are carried out. These include:

- isolation of non-conforming product,
- labelling of non-conforming product,
- completion of Non-conformity Reports,
- decisions on subsequent actions,
- rejection procedures,
- inspection and test of repaired/reworked product,
- use of non-conforming product under concession,
- keeping and maintenance of records.

It is the responsibility of the quality manager and all departmental managers and supervisors to ensure that the procedures in PROC-07 are followed.

ATMOSTAT CONTROLS LTD
QUALITY MANUAL

|21. CORRECTIVE AND PREVENTIVE ACTION (Issue 2, Dec. 1994)

Full details, including causes, of any material non-conformity are included in the Non-conformity report, which is circulated to all departments concerned.

21.1 IMMEDIATE CORRECTIVE ACTION

The appropriate action necessary to remove the cause of the non-conformity will be initiated, recorded and followed through to a satisfactory conclusion by the quality control department.

|21.2 PREVENTIVE ACTION

Analysis of non-conformities takes place in order to instigate actions to prevent recurrences of defects. These actions and the performance of products in the field, along with customer complaints, are monitored and recorded to detect trends and identify problems and further corrective actions required.

The quality manager and departmental managers and supervisors meet at regular intervals to review long-term and short-term corrective and preventive actions, to evaluate their effectiveness.

|21.3 COMPLAINTS PROCEDURE

All customer complaints are processed by the sales department. It is that department's job to record complaints and communicate them to the relevant areas of manufacture and/or quality control to ensure that action is taken to improve the manufacturing and quality control standards.

A record is maintained of all complaints. The quality control department analyses the quantity and nature of complaints on a monthly basis, and makes this information available to the company management review meetings.

Changes in Issue 2: Title changed and section 21.2, 'Preventive Action' added in line with changes to Standard, 1994; original section 21.2 renumbered 21.3.

| Ref: QM-01 | Issue: 3 Feb. 1995 | Page: 22 of 27 |

ATMOSTAT CONTROLS LTD
QUALITY MANUAL

22. HANDLING, STORAGE, PACKAGING AND DELIVERY
(Issue 1, July 1993)

22.1 HANDLING

The handling of all materials and products is in accordance with:

- requirements identified on packaging,
- the procedures specified in the appropriate manuals,
- standard practice with regard to health and safety.

22.2 STORAGE

The storage of all materials and products is in accordance with PROC-08, Warehousing and Distribution Procedures, section 1, including:

- storage in appropriate areas,
- protection from damage and deterioration,
- stock control procedures,
- stock rotation procedures.

22.3 PACKAGING

The packaging of all products is in accordance with PROC-04, Production Procedures, and PROC-08, Warehousing and Distribution Procedures, section 2, including:

- release from final inspection,
- protection from damage and deterioration,
- special customer requirements,
- labelling.

22.4 DELIVERY

The delivery of products is in accordance with PROC-08, Warehousing and Distribution Procedures, section 3, including:

- protection from damage and deterioration,
- special customer requirements,
- labelling.

ATMOSTAT CONTROLS LTD
QUALITY MANUAL

23. QUALITY RECORDS (Issue 1, July 1993)

All records used to control product quality are retained in an acceptable manner, i.e. legibly and readily retrievable.

Records are maintained and stored in accordance with the master list kept by the quality manager, which identifies:

- record title,
- reference code/number,
- revision status,
- department(s) responsible for maintenance,
- storage location,
- minimum period for retention.

Records are stored at source until their immediate use has been exhausted (or the retention period has been exceeded), after which they are archived by the appropriate department.

No records may be destroyed without the approval of the managing director.

ATMOSTAT CONTROLS LTD
QUALITY MANUAL

24. INTERNAL QUALITY AUDITING (Issue 1, July 1993)

Internal quality system audits take place on a planned basis in accordance with PROC-09, Internal Quality Audits. These procedures include:

- objectives of internal audits,
- planning of audits,
- audit frequency,
- responsible auditors,
- departments to be audited,
- scope of audits,
- auditing procedure,
- audit reports,
- corrective actions,
- audit follow-up.

ATMOSTAT CONTROLS LTD
QUALITY MANUAL

25. EMPLOYEE TRAINING (Issue 1, July 1993)

Following satisfactory completion of the interview process, new employees are introduced to the company structure, rules and layout. An appropriate induction programme, depending on the employee's function, is devised by the department manager and training manager and followed.

The first three months with the company are regarded as a probationary period, during which time the employee is given full job and quality training. A record is kept of all work carried out, details of problems encountered, and supervisor's comments. At the end of this time this log is examined by the department head. On the basis of the record, the individual's capabilities and suitability for the job are evaluated.

The training needs of all employees are continually kept under review and revised as necessary. The department manager and supervisors are responsible for identifying the training needs of individuals, and the former, along with the training manager, are responsible for the facilitation of the appropriate training.

On-going training is given to individuals whose performance fails to reach the required standard.

All employees are continually updated on the company's quality programmes, and the importance of their individual contribution to product quality.

Full advantages are taken of any relevant training courses, and the skills acquired are passed on to other members who may benefit from this knowledge.

Training records are maintained by departmental heads.

ATMOSTAT CONTROLS LTD
QUALITY MANUAL

26. SERVICING (Issue 1, July 1993)

Installation and servicing of the company's products is carried out in accordance with PROC-10, After-sales Servicing, which includes:

- installation procedures,
- planned maintenance procedures,
- repair procedures,
- call-out logging and routing procedures,
- equipment requirements,
- references to calibration procedures,
- standards for engineer response times,
- repair standards,
- technical references,
- references to spare parts and accessories lists.

It is the responsibility of the technical director and the service manager to ensure that these procedures are followed.

27. STATISTICAL TECHNIQUES (Issue 1, July 1993)

Statistical techniques are used in all relevant areas of data analysis in connection with process control, and are as detailed in PROC-04, Production Procedures.

It is the responsibility of the production director to ensure that all statistical techniques are appropriate to the products and processes to which they are applied.

ATMOSTAT CONTROLS LTD
CONTROL OF NON-CONFORMING PRODUCT

THIS IS A CONTROLLED DOCUMENT AND NOT TO BE COPIED WITHOUT AUTHORISATION FROM THE QUALITY MANAGER. ONLY ORIGINALS, SIGNED BY THE MANAGING DIRECTOR, MAY BE USED AS WORKING DOCUMENTS.

CONTENTS

	Section	Page	Issue
Introduction	1	2	1
Identification and isolation of non-conforming product	2	3	1
Disposition of non-conforming product	3	5	1
Records	4	7	1

Appendices:

NCPL-01	Non-conforming Product Label
SCRL-01	Scrap Label
NCR-01	Non-conformity Report
WI-07-01	Work instruction: Completing the Non-conformity Report
WAN-01	Weekly Analysis of Non-conformities

Revision notes:

Page 2, section 1.3, Reference changed from BS 5750, part 1, 1987, to BS EN ISO 9001, 1994 (Dec. 1994).

This procedures manual has been approved by:_____

Date:_____

Ref: PROC-07	Issue: 1 Dec. 1993	Page: 1 of 7

ATMOSTAT CONTROLS LTD
CONTROL OF NON-CONFORMING PRODUCT

1. INTRODUCTION

1.1 SCOPE

This manual describes the procedures used by Atmostat Controls Ltd in the identification, isolation and disposition of any material or product not conforming to the appropriate requirements.

Its purpose is to ensure that only materials and products that meet the required specifications are used in the production or other processes or delivered to customers.

1.2 DEFINITION

Non-conforming product is defined as any raw material, part-processed material or product, or finished product that fails to meet the specified requirements following inspection or test as laid down in PROC-05, Inspection and Testing.

1.3 REFERENCES

BS EN ISO 9001, 1994, clause 4.13.

1.4 RESPONSIBILITY

It is the responsibility of the quality manager and the inspectors and testers of the quality control department to ensure that the following procedures are implemented, and that consequent actions are followed through to satisfactory conclusions.

ATMOSTAT CONTROLS LTD
CONTROL OF NON-CONFORMING PRODUCT

2. IDENTIFICATION AND ISOLATION OF NON-CONFORMING PRODUCT

2.1 IDENTIFICATION

2.1.1 Inspection and test procedures are described in PROC-05, Inspection and Testing.

2.1.2 In the event of any material failing to meet the specified requirements, it is immediately classified as 'non-conforming product'.

2.1.3 Non-conforming Product labels (NCPL-01) are attached to individual items, or, in the case of smaller individual items or batches of smaller items, to the box or container in which they are situated.

The labels are clearly marked with the number of the corresponding Non-conformity report to be raised.

The labels are firmly fixed to prevent accidental removal, and remain in place until the product has been redesignated as conforming, or the decision implemented to return to the supplier, scrap, rework/repair or use under concession.

2.2 INITIATION OF NON-CONFORMING PRODUCT REPORT

2.2.1 The inspector, tester, or other person identifying the product as non-conforming, completes section A of the Non-conformity Report, NCPR-01, in accordance with Work Instruction WI-07-01, Completing the Non-conformity Report.

2.2.2 The Non-conformity Report is filed in numerical order in the originating department's 'Non-conformity Reports, Open' file.

ATMOSTAT CONTROLS LTD
CONTROL OF NON-CONFORMING PRODUCT

2. IDENTIFICATION AND ISOLATION OF NON-CONFORMING PRODUCT (cont.)

2.3 ISOLATION

2.3.1 Having been identified as non-conforming, all such material is moved immediately into the appropriate non-conforming product area. These are located:

- in the receiving inspection bay (for raw materials and bought-in components);
- next to canteen in production area 1 (for printed circuit boards and sub-assemblies);
- next to supervisor's office in production area 2 (for main assemblies);
- in the final inspection bay (for completed product failing final inspection).

2.3.2 The non-conforming product areas are clearly marked as to their purpose. No material other than non-conforming is permitted to be stored in these areas.

2.3.3 No non-conforming product is permitted in any place other than the designated non-conforming product area, except for the purposes of:

- identification;
- transit to or from that area;
- evaluation for disposition decisions;
- rework or repair;
- use under authorised concession;

or otherwise by the authority of the quality manager or his/her deputies.

2.3.4 An exception to 2.3.1 and 2.3.3 may be made in the case of large or bulky items that it is not practical to store in the non-conforming product areas. In this case they are clearly identified to prevent their use as conforming product and isolated from any conforming product.

ATMOSTAT CONTROLS LTD
CONTROL OF NON-CONFORMING PRODUCT

3. DISPOSITION OF NON-CONFORMING PRODUCT

3.1 The inspection supervisor reviews the open Non-conformity Reports daily, or more frequently if necessary, to determine the disposition of non-conforming product. He/she will involve the purchasing and production managers and/or supervisors if necessary.

3.2 The decision will be made to do one of the following.

  3.2.1 Return material to the supplier.
  3.2.2 Scrap the material or product.
  3.2.3 Return the product to production for rework or repair.
  3.2.4 Seek authority from the quality manager to use the material or product under concession.

3.3 The decision made is recorded on the Non-conformity Report, NCR-01, in accordance with Work Instruction WI-07-01, Completing the Non-conformity Report.

3.4 In the case of 3.2.1, a photocopy of the Non-conformity Report is sent to the purchasing department, to be dealt with in accordance with the procedures in PROC-03, Purchasing, section 5, Returning defective material to supplier.

3.5 In the case of 3.2.2, Scrap labels (SCRL-01) are attached to individual items, or, in the case of smaller individual items or batches of smaller items, to the box or container in which they are situated.

The scrap material is placed in the scrap bay. Its removal and/or disposal is only by the authority of the quality manager.

A photocopy of the Non-conformity Report is sent to the quality manager, who informs the purchasing or production manager as appropriate.

The quality manager, with the assistance of the purchasing or production manager as appropriate, authorises the eventual disposal of the non-conforming product, and completes the Non-conformity Report in accordance with Work Instruction WI-07-01, Completing the Non-conformity Report.

ATMOSTAT CONTROLS LTD
CONTROL OF NON-CONFORMING PRODUCT

3. DISPOSITION OF NON-CONFORMING PRODUCT (cont.)

3.6 In the case of 3.2.3, a photocopy of the Non-conformity Report is sent to the production manager, who arranges for the product to be removed from the non-conforming product area and reworked or repaired accordingly.

When rework or repairs have been completed, the production supervisor completes the relevant section of the Non-conformity Report in accordance with Work Instruction WI-07-01, Completing the Non-conformity Report.

All repaired and reworked product is reinspected and/or retested in full in accordance with the appropriate procedures for that product. Only when the product has satisfactorily passed inspection and test may the Non-conforming Product labels be removed, and the inspector/tester complete section C of the Non-conformity Report in accordance with Work Instruction WI-07-01, Completing the Non-conformity Report.

3.7 In the case of 3.2.4, the quality manager must seek the approval of the customer before authorising the use of non-conforming product under concession. The customer must provide agreement in writing, and reference to this agreement is quoted on Certificates of Conformity covering deliveries containing the permitted deviation, as detailed in PROC-01, Contract Review, section 8, Permitted deviations.

Following receipt of agreement from the customer, the quality manager notes the batch numbers of the material or product for entry on the Certificates of Conformity, and authorises the removal of the Non-conforming Product labels and the further processing or delivery of the product as appropriate.

The quality manager completes section C of the Non-conformity Report in accordance with Work Instruction WI-07-01, Completing the Non-conformity Report.

ATMOSTAT CONTROLS LTD
CONTROL OF NON-CONFORMING PRODUCT

4. RECORDS

4.1 Non-conformity Reports are completed in accordance with the above procedures and Work Instruction WI-07-01, Completing the Non-conformity Report.

4.2 The Non-conformity Report original is filed in the originating department's 'Non-conformity Reports, Open' file until all the specified decisions and actions have been taken and the report signed off as being complete by the quality manager or his/her deputy. It is then filed in the originating department's 'Non-conformity Reports, Closed' file.

4.3 Purchasing, production, or other departments receiving photocopies of Non-conformity Reports file them in originating department and numerical order.

4.4 All originals and copies of Non-conformity Reports are kept for a minimum of three years from the date on which they were closed off, and are dealt with in accordance with section 23 of the quality manual, Quality Records.

NON-CONFORMING PRODUCT

NO.   OF QTY.

NON-CONFORMITY REPORT NO.

THIS LABEL IS NOT TO BE REMOVED WITHOUT
THE QUALITY MANAGER'S AUTHORITY

Ref: NCPL-01   Issue 1, November 1993

SCRAP   DO NOT USE

Ref: SCRL-01   Issue 1, November 1993

ATMOSTAT CONTROLS LTD
NON-CONFORMITY REPORT

A | ORIGINATING DEPARTMENT: | REPORT NO:

PRODUCT DETAILS: DESCRIPTION:

CODE: | BATCH: | QTY ON THIS REPORT

DETAILS OF NON-CONFORMITY:

SIGNED BY: (INSPECTOR/TESTER) DATE:

B | CORRECTIVE ACTION PROPOSED:

RETURN TO SUPPLIER (copy of report to purchasing)
SCRAP (copy of report to quality manager)
REPAIR/REWORK (copy of report to production)
USE UNDER CONCESSION (copy of report to quality manager)

SIGNED BY: (SUPERVISOR)   DATE:

C | CORRECTIVE ACTION TAKEN:

SIGNED BY: POSITION: DATE:

D | THE ABOVE ACTION HAS BEEN SATISFACTORILY COMPLETED:

SIGNED BY: (QUALITY MANAGER)   DATE:

Ref: NCR-01, Issue 1, December 1993

ATMOSTAT CONTROLS LTD
WORK INSTRUCTION

COMPLETING THE NON-CONFORMITY REPORT

For use by: Quality manager and deputies,
inspectors and testers; Receiving, In-process and Final;
departmental managers and supervisors.

Location: Receiving, In-process and Final Inspection areas,
Production Office,
Purchasing Office.

1. INSPECTORS AND TESTERS

1.1 The inspector or tester identifies a material or product not conforming to the specified requirements, and follows the procedures detailed in PROC-07, Control of Non-conforming Product.

1.2 The next consecutive number for the department is entered on the Non-conforming Product Label and the Non-conformity Report.

1.3 The originating department is entered on section A of the Non-conformity Report, i.e. Receiving/In-process/Final Inspection, or other.

1.4 The description, code and batch number (if applicable) are entered on section A of the Non-conformity Report, along with details of the non-conformity and the quantity of items included in the report.

1.5 The inspector or tester signs and dates section A of the report and files it in numerical order in the department's 'Non-conformity Reports, Open' file, awaiting inspection by the department's supervisor.

2. INSPECTION/TEST SUPERVISOR

2.1 The supervisor reviews the Non-conformity Reports daily, or more frequently as necessary, and determines, in conjuction with purchasing or production supervisors and/or managers and the quality manager as appropriate, the course of action to be followed.

2.2 Details of the decided action are entered by the supervisor in section B, and the appropriate box ticked.

2.3 Section B is signed and dated by the supervisor, who then forwards a photocopy of the Non-conformity Report to the appropriate manager.

Ref: WI-07-01   Issue: 2 Dec. 1993   Page: 1 of 2

ATMOSTAT CONTROLS LTD
WORK INSTRUCTION

COMPLETING THE NON-CONFORMITY REPORT (cont.)

3. MANAGERS RECEIVING COPIES OF NON-CONFORMITY REPORTS

3.1 The departmental manager, having arranged for the necessary action to be completed, completes section C of the Non-conformity Report copy, signs and dates it, and files it in numerical order in his/her department.

3.2 The departmental manager also completes the details as in 3.1 in section C of the original in the originating department.

4. QUALITY MANAGER

4.1 The quality manager or his/her deputy reviews at least once per week the Non-conformity Reports in the 'Open' files in all departments, extracting the details for entry onto the Weekly Analysis of Non-conformities, WAN-01.

4.2 When satisfied that the corrective actions have been taken as proposed, the quality manager (or deputy) signs and dates section D of the original Non-conformity Report, and gives instructions for it to be filed numerically in the originating department's 'Non-conformity Reports, Closed' file.

ATMOSTAT CONTROLS LTD WEEK NO:_____19____

WEEKLY ANALYSIS OF NON-CONFORMITIES

QUANTITY OF NON-CONFORMITIES	RET. TO SUPPLIER	SCRAP	REPAIR REWORK	USE u. CONCESN
A RECEIVING INSPECTION				
Electronic components				
MPUs				
Sub-assemblies				
Cabinets				
Printed circuit boards				
Thermostats				
Humidistats				
Temperature probes				
Humidity detectors				
Hardware and fittings				
SUB-TOTAL				
B IN-PROCESS CONTROL, Production Area 1				
Temperature control modules				
Humidity control modules				
MPU boards				
Control units				
SUB-TOTAL				
C IN-PROCESS CONTROL, Production Area 2				
Temperature control units				
Humidity control units				
Master control units				
Cabinets				
SUB-TOTAL				
D FINAL INSPECTION				
Temperature control units				
Humidity control units				
Master control units				
Cabinets				
Packaging				
Paperwork				
SUB-TOTAL				
TOT. NON-CONFORMITIES				

Ref: WAN-01, Issue 1, December 1993

ATMOSTAT CONTROLS LTD
INSPECTION AND TESTING

THIS IS A CONTROLLED DOCUMENT AND NOT TO BE COPIED WITHOUT AUTHORISATION FROM THE QUALITY MANAGER. ONLY ORIGINALS, SIGNED BY THE MANAGING DIRECTOR, MAY BE USED AS WORKING DOCUMENTS.

CONTENTS

	Section	Page	Issue
Introduction	0	2	1
Receiving inspection and testing	2	3	1
In-process inspection and testing	3	[*Not included*]	
Final inspection and testing	4	[*Not included*]	
Records	5	[*Not included*]	

Appendices:

ITP-3009   Inspection/Test Procedure, Control Cabinet AB-3
ITP-5122   Inspection/Test Procedure, TP21c Temperature Probe
[*In practice, the list of Inspection/Test Procedures is likely to be very long, and would constitute an appendix item in itself.*]
RIREP-01   Receiving Inspection Report

Revision notes:

Page 2, section 1.2, Reference changed from BS 5750, part 1, 1987, to BS EN 9001, 1994 (Dec. 1994).

This procedures manual has been approved by:_____

                                                    Date:_____

| Ref: PROC-05 | Issue: 1 Jan. 1994 | Page: 1 of XX |

ATMOSTAT CONTROLS LTD
INSPECTION AND TESTING

1. INTRODUCTION

1.1 SCOPE

This manual describes the procedures used by Atmostat Controls Ltd in the inspection and testing of purchased materials and finished products, and the in-process inspections and tests.

Its purpose is to ensure that only materials and products that meet the required specifications are used in the production or other processes or delivered to customers.

1.2 REFERENCES

BS EN ISO 9001, 1994, clause 4.10.

1.4 RESPONSIBILITY

It is the responsibility of the quality manager and the inspectors and testers of the quality control department to ensure that the following procedures are implemented, and that consequent actions are followed through to satisfactory conclusions.

ATMOSTAT CONTROLS LTD
INSPECTION AND TESTING

2. RECEIVING INSPECTION

2.1 All purchased material is subjected to inspection and/or testing before being released for processing, with the only exception as in 2.10.

2.2 All delivered material is placed in the goods inward bay, where it is checked for compliance with the delivery note and the purchase order in accordance with PROC-08, Warehousing and Distribution Procedures, before being accepted and placed in the 'awaiting inspection' area.

2.3 No material is removed from the 'awaiting inspection' area until immediately prior to its being required for inspection/testing, subject to the exception in 2.10.

2.4 Materials are inspected and/or tested in accordance with the appropriate Raw Material Specification, RMSPEC-01, etc. and Inspection/Test procedures (ITP sheets) as follows:

- Electronic components   ITP-000–ITP-999
- Microprocessor units   ITP-1000–ITP-1999
- Sub-assemblies   ITP-2000–ITP-2999
- Cabinets   ITP-3000–ITP-3999
- Printed circuit boards   ITP-4000–ITP-4999
- Thermostats and temperature probes   ITP-5000–ITP-5999
- Humidistats and humidity detectors   ITP-6000–ITP-6999
- Miscellaneous components   ITP-7000–ITP-7999.

2.5 The ITP sheets give the sample percentage of the total order to be inspected/tested in the first instance as the 'first level inspection'. If that sample fails the inspection/test, the ITP sheet will indicate whether further sampling is to take place or the entire order is to be rejected.

2.6 Any material failing to meet the specified requirements is dealt with in accordance with PROC-07, Control of Non-conforming Product.

2.7 On satisfactory completion of inspection/testing, each item, or container or box of items in the case of smaller items, is marked with the individual inspector's passed/date stamp in accordance with the relevant ITP sheet.

ATMOSTAT CONTROLS LTD
INSPECTION AND TESTING

2. RECEIVING INSPECTION (cont.)

2.8   The inspector completes the Receiving Inspection Report, RIREP-01, for each batch of material inspected or tested, indicating the code and description of the item, the quantity delivered, the percentage inspected, the quantities accepted and rejected, the Non-conformity Report number (if applicable), and adds his/her signature. A new report is commenced daily.

2.9   The material having passed inspection/testing, is passed to the components store in accordance with PROC-08, Warehousing and Distribution Procedures, section 2.

2.10   In the case of urgent need by production, material may bypass the receiving inspection process, but only with the approval of the quality manager, who will use his/her discretion in the giving of approval depending on the type of material and the supplier's record of providing defect-free deliveries. Batch numbers of uninspected material must be recorded against batch numbers of product by the production manager in case of defects arising later. (See PROC-04, Production Procedures, section 4, Process control.)

[By now the reader should have a good understanding of the format of procedure manuals, so we will not take this one any further.

In this case, work instructions have been combined with material specifications into 'Inspection/test procedures'. The exact format is not rigid, but must be appropriate to the needs of the organisation. Note that reference is made to specifications if they are not quoted in the inspection/test procedures, and the acceptance criteria and tolerances of measurements are given.]

ATMOSTAT CONTROLS LTD
INSPECTION/TEST PROCEDURE

CONTROL CABINET, AB-3

For use by: Receiving inspectors
Location: Receiving inspection area

SUPPLIER   ACME ALUMINIUM LTD, HIGHTOWN.

SPECIFICATIONS   1.2 mm cabinet with hinged front door, painted grey.
                     Fully specified on drawing ACME.L123, issue 3, Oct. 1993.

FIRST LEVEL INSPECTION   10% of delivered lot. If any one failure in 10%
                          sample, then inspect 100%.

EQUIPMENT REQUIRED   Standard steel 1 m rule, XK55 jig, calibrated
                          micrometer, AB-3 reference sample, cotton
                          glove.

INSPECTION PROCEDURE

1 Remove protective wrapping and set aside for re-use.

2 Check that the external cabinet dimensions are as per drawing, within the
   tolerances given, as measured with a standard steel rule.

3 Check the positions of the mounting holes using the XK55 jig. If the jig fits all
   the holes without significant side movement, mounting holes are acceptable.

4 Check the operation of lock. Key should turn easily and door should not move
   when closed.

5 Check that all metal edges are smooth by running a cotton-gloved finger along
   them. Edges are satisfactory if no cotton fibres are picked up.

6 Check that paint colour is in accordance with the AB-3 reference sample; a
   shade lighter than sample is acceptable, darker is not.

7 Check thickness of paint by measuring with a calibrated micrometer the
   thickness of the front panel in three places. Acceptable thickness is in the
   range 1.30–1.38 mm.

8 Check for obvious paint defects, e.g. 'orange peel', scratches, surface
   abrasion, etc.

9 If cabinet meets with requirements, apply passed/date stamp to inner door, top
   left-hand corner, and rewrap in original wrappings. Apply AB-3 label to top of
   wrapped cabinet and stamp label with passed/date stamp.

Ref: ITP-3009   Issue: 1 Dec. 1993   Page: 1 of 1

ATMOSTAT CONTROLS LTD
INSPECTION/TEST PROCEDURE

TP21c TEMPERATURE PROBE

For use by: Receiving inspectors
Location: Receiving inspection area

SUPPLIER   CADWALLEDER COMPONENTS LTD, LOWVILLE.

SPECIFICATIONS   152 mm long by 3 mm diameter immersible probe.
                  Fully specified on Cadwalleder's data sheet TP21c/93.

FIRST LEVEL INSPECTION   3% of delivered lot. If any one failure in 3%
                          sample, entire lot to be rejected.

EQUIPMENT REQUIRED   AC707 jig, calibrated Exco 115 digital multimeter,
                      test oven and refrigerator, two calibrated glass
                      thermometers.

INSPECTION PROCEDURE

1 Pass the TP21c probe right through the tube in the AC707 jig. If it passes
  completely through without obstruction it is sufficiently straight and of acceptable diameter.

2 Set the test oven to +80 degrees Celsius and the refrigerator to +5 degrees,
  allow each to stabilise for 20 minutes. Using calibrated glass thermometers
  check temperature in the range +77–+83 degrees in the oven and +3 –+7 in
  the bottom of the refrigerator. Adjust if necessary, allow to stabilise for 5
  minutes and check temperatures again.

3 Connect the Exco 115 multimeter leads together. Set the multimeter to ohms
  × 1 range. Adjust meter zero control to read 0 +/−0.

5 Place the TP21c probes in the oven with their leads passing through the door
  seal, allow temperature to stabilise for 5 minutes and measure the resistance
  of each. It should be in the range 98–106 ohms. Leave in place for one hour
  and measure again; it should be still in the same range.

6 Remove the TP21c probes from the oven, allow to cool for 5 minutes and place
  in the bottom of the refrigerator with their leads passing through the door seal.
  Allow temperature to stabilise for 5 minutes and measure the resistance of
  each. It should be in the range 3,100–3,400 ohms. Leave in place for one hour
  and measure again; it should be still in the same range.

7 If these tests on the 3 per cent sample are satisfactory, repack them into their
  respective boxes and apply passed/date stamp to each box lid in the lot.

| Ref: ITP-5112 | Issue: 1 Dec. 1993 | Page: 1 of 1 |

ATMOSTAT CONTROLS LTD

RECEIVING INSPECTION REPORT

DATE:

| PRODUCT | | | % | QUANTITY | | | N.C.R. | Signed |
CODE	SUPPLIER	DESCRIPTION	INSP.	TOTAL	ACCEPTED	REJECTED	REP. NO.	INSPECTOR

Ref: RIREP-01, Issue 1, September 1993

ATMOSTAT CONTROLS LTD	NO:	94/0823
CONTRACT REVIEW RECORD	RETAIN IN CUSTOMER FILE	

CUSTOMER:	EXISTING: yes	QUOTE NO: 94/0753	REPEAT	Y
European Aerospace Plc	NEW:	ORDER NO: pending	ORDER?	N

ARE CHANGES REQUIRED TO EXISTING DETAILS OR SPECIFICATIONS? (Y/N) | Y |

BRIEF DETAILS OF REQUIREMENTS, INCLUDING REFERENCES TO
SPECIFICATIONS OR CHANGES TO SPECIFICATIONS:

35 off Mark–II Total Environment Controllers
Extended humidity and temperature ranges, as detailed in Customers'
Specification sheet 93–A/1006c.
Added frost control down to minus 30 degrees Celsius.

IF NOT EXISTING PRODUCTS, SUMMARY OF ESTIMATED REQUIREMENTS

	REQ Y/N	DETAILS INCLUDING TIMESCALES	SIGNED BY MANAGER	APPROVED BY CLIENT DATE	SALES MGR
DESIGN & PROVING	Y	Ranges/Frost control, 8 wks.	*P.J.M.*	9/10/94	*J.V.*
PROCUREMENT	N				
PRODUCTION	Y	Train operatives, 2 wks.	*J.I.*	N/A	
TESTING	Y	Soak-test for 4 wks.	*J.S.*	9/10/94	*J.V.*
DELIVERY	Y	Req. by 1 April 1995		7/11/94	*J.V.*
INSTALLATION	N				
SERVICING	Y	Add to existing contract	*A.T.*	15/11/94	

NOTES:

Delivery deadline is 1 April 1995, but customer will accept delivery
any time after 10 March 1995.
We should aim for production during January, subject to signed contract.
                    J.V., 1/12/1994

DATE OF FINAL AGREEMENT	REF:	SALES MGR:
WITH CUSTOMER OF ALL DETAILS: 6/12/94	Letter	*J.V.*

CREV-01, Issue 1, December 1993

ATMOSTAT CONTROLS LTD

CALIBRATION RECORD

EQUIPMENT DESCRIPTION:	MODEL NO:	ABC 700
Gramco Digital Scale	SERIAL NO:	100367
	LOCATION:	Rec. Inspection
	FIRST USED	13 March 1994
CALIBRATION PROCEDURE:	REF NO:	WI–06–17
In accordance with Work Inst. WI–06–19		
	FREQUENCY	Monthly

PERMISSIBLE TOLERANCES: +/– 0.1 gm.

DATE	ACCURACY FOUND	ADJUST-MENT	ACCURACY LEFT	COMMENTS	SIGNED ENGINEER
12.03.94	+0.03 gm	NONE	+0.03 gm		MGM
10.04.94	+0.04 gm	NONE	+0.04 gm		MGM
10.05.94	+0.08 gm	CALIB	+0.02 gm		MGM
09.06.94	–0.01 gm	NONE	–0.01 gm		MGM
08.07.94	–0.16 gm	CALIB	+0.03 gm	Informed quality manager	MGM
10.08.94	–0.09 gm	CALIB	–0.06 gm	Gain control near maximum	MGM
17.08.94	–0.13 gm			Informed quality manager	
		Taken out of service for repair			MGM
03.10.94	+0.01 gm	NONE	+0.01 gm	Returned after repair	MGM
02.11.94	+0.02 gm	NONE	+0.02 gm		MGM
01.12.94	–0.03 gm	NONE	–0.03 gm		MGM
03.01.95	–0.06 gm	CALIB	–0.01 gm		MGM

NOTE TO READER: The calibration record shows that the scale was out of calibration on 8 July. It was necessary to inform the quality manager, as any measurements made with this equipment since the last calibration could have been erroneous, and the quality manager would have to determine the implications of this.

The scale was again giving trouble on 17 August, so it was taken out of service. Again, the quality manager would need to be informed so he/she could take the appropriate action.

Ref: CALIB-01, Issue 1, 1 January 1993

ATMOSTAT CONTROLS LTD
DEPARTMENT TRAINING PLAN

DEPT:	Production Area 1
MGR:	Jim Ikan	DATE:	3/7/94

T–Training need identified
C–Training/retraining completed (see individual training records)
R–Retraining need identified

DEPARTMENT STAFF / TRAINING COURSE	Bob Jones	Brian Smith	Ann White	George Tucker	Julie Mason	Freda Thompson	Mike Ashwood	Simon Small
Basic Quality System Trng	T C	T C	T C	R C	T C	T C	T C	T C
N.C.P. Procedures	T C	T C	T C	R	T	T C	T C	T
Resistor colour codes	T C		T	T	T	T C	T C	T C
Lead-out forming	T C		T	T	T	T C	T C	T C
Flow-soldering	T C		T	T	T	T C	T C	T C
Microchip handling	T C		T C	T	R	T C	T C	T
Stores requisitions		T C	T	T	T	T	T C	
Packing circuit boards	T C	T C	T	T	T	T C	R C	T
Staff supervision I			T C		T		T	
Staff supervision II			T C		T		T	
Fork lift truck cert.	T C	T C					T	
Health & Safety I	T C	T C	T	T	T	T C	T C	T C
Health & Safety II	T C	T	T				T C	
Inspection	T		T C		T	T	T C	

Ref: DTRP-01, Issue 2, October 1992   Page: 1   of: 1

ATMOSTAT CONTROLS LTD   TRAINING RECORD

NAME:	·Ann White		JOB TITLE:	Production supervisor
DEPT:	Prod. Area 1		MANAGER:	Jim Ikan

TRAINING RECEIVED	DATE	INT/EXT	TRAINER	COMMENTS
Resistor colour codes	21.03.88	INT	J.G.H.	
Lead-out forming	22.03.88	INT	J.G.H.	
Flow-soldering	03.04.88	INT	J.G.H.	
Stores requisitions	21.06.89	INT	J.G.H.	
Packing circuit boards	14.10.90	INT	F.S.	
Health & Safety I	08.11.90	EXT	COL of FE	Certificate gained
Inspection	28.05.91	INT	J.S.	Excellent grasp of quality
Microchip handling	07.09.91	INT	F.S.	
Staff supervision I	02.02.92	EXT	HI-TRAIN	Cert. w, credit gained; should go for SS II! J.S.
Basic Quality System	09.10.92	INT	J.S.	
N.C.P. Procedures	19.01.93	INT	J.S.	
Staff supervision II	21.09.94	EXT	HI-TRAIN	Cert. w. credit gained

Ref: TRREC-01, Issue 2, October 1992 PAGE: 1 of: 1

ATMOSTAT CONTROLS LTD   SERVICE CALL LOG   DATE: 6 January 1995

CUSTOMER: Rainbow Ltd **PASSED TO:** J. Black
EQUIPMENT: Refrigeration **COMMENTS:**
SERVICE REQ.: Not maintaining temperature

	DATE	TIME	RESPONSE TIME
RECEIVED	6/1	09.30	TO
PASSED	6/1	09.50	ARRIVAL 02.15
ON SITE	6/1	11.45	TO
COMPLETE	6/1	13.30	COMPLETE 04.00

CUSTOMER: European Aero. **PASSED TO:** S. Green
EQUIPMENT: Mk II Controller **COMMENTS:** New transformer req–call back tomorrow
SERVICE REQ.: Keeps blowing fuses

	DATE	TIME	RESPONSE TIME
RECEIVED	6/1	10.15	TO
PASSED	6/1	10.30	ARRIVAL 02.15
ON SITE	6/1	12.30	TO
COMPLETE	7/1	09.30	COMPLETE 07.15

CUSTOMER: Smith Anderson **PASSED TO:** J. Black
EQUIPMENT: Warehouse system **COMMENTS:**
SERVICE REQ.: Leaking water URGENT

	DATE	TIME	RESPONSE TIME
RECEIVED	6/1	10.30	TO
PASSED	6/1	10.40	ARRIVAL 04.15
ON SITE	6/1	14.45	TO
COMPLETE	6/1	15.35	COMPLETE 05.05

CUSTOMER: Bloggs Dairy Prods. **PASSED TO:** T. White
EQUIPMENT: Cold room **COMMENTS:** Oiled fan; return to fit new motor
SERVICE REQ.: Noisy fan

	DATE	TIME	RESPONSE TIME
RECEIVED	6/1	11.15	TO
PASSED	6/1	11.25	ARRIVAL 04.15
ON SITE	6/1	15.30	TO
COMPLETE	8/1	10.10	COMPLETE 14.45

CUSTOMER: Quality Papers Ltd. **PASSED TO:** S. Green
EQUIPMENT: Warehouse system **COMMENTS:** Tested system, no fault found
SERVICE REQ.: 1 humidifier not working

	DATE	TIME	RESPONSE TIME
RECEIVED	6/1	16.40	TO
PASSED	6/1	16.50	ARRIVAL 01.40
ON SITE	7/1	10.20	TO
COMPLETE	7/1	11.10	COMPLETE 02.30

CUSTOMER: **PASSED TO:**
EQUIPMENT: **COMMENTS:**
SERVICE REQ.:

	DATE	TIME	RESPONSE TIME
RECEIVED			TO
PASSED			ARRIVAL
ON SITE			TO
COMPLETE			COMPLETE

Response times based on 8-hour working day 9.00 – 17.00

Ref: SCL-01, Issue 3, September 1993

ATMOSTAT CONTROLS LTD	DATE:	12/01/95
	NO:	95/009
CUSTOMER COMPLAINT	TAKEN BY:	Sue Booker

CUSTOMER DETAILS:
> Charles Winnett, (Engineering manager)
> European Aerospace Plc,
> Anytown.
> Tel: 565678 ext. 456

PRODUCT REFERENCE:
> Mark II Controllers (22 off)

SERIAL/BATCH NUMBERS:
> Serial numbers A86/23441 thro' 23462

DESPATCH DETAILS:
> Customer order number EAP–2953, dated 4 August 1994,
> Delivered 11 October 1994

NATURE OF COMPLAINT:

> Of the 22 units delivered, 13 have developed stiff
> door locks, 4 of which are impossible to open.

> URGENT ACTION IS REQUIRED.

PASSED FOR ACTION:
> Alan Tinker, Service manager

ACTION TAKEN:
> Contacted customer. Agreed to replace all 22 locks.
> Locks replaced on 14 January 1995

ACTION TAKEN BY: *A.T.*   DATE 14/1/95

FOLLOW-UP ACTION:
> Customer Services rang Mr Winnett to check if all OK.
> Mr Winnett was delighted with service.

FOLLOW-UP ACTION TAKEN BY: *Jane Spigget*   DATE 18/1/95

Ref: CCFM-01, Issue 1, August 1993

ATMOSTAT CONTROLS LTD
SUPPLIER ASSESSMENT QUESTIONNAIRE

COMPANY NAME:	POST CODE:
ADDRESS:	TEL. NO:
	FAX NO:

NATURE/TYPE OF BUSINESS	PRODUCTS/SERVICES:

NUMBERS OF STAFF EMPLOYED:	TOTAL:	
	PRODUCTION/SERVICE PROVISION:	
	INSPECTION/QUALITY CONTROL:	

SENIOR EXECUTIVE ON SITE:	POSITION:

NAMES OF PRINCIPAL PEOPLE RESPONSIBLE FOR:	QUALITY CONTROL:
	SALES:
	TECHNICAL SERVICE:
	DELIVERIES:

IS THE ORGANISATION APPROVED TO
BS 5750/ISO 9000 OR A SIMILAR STANDARD?   [YES | NO]

IF YES, PLEASE STATE:

STANDARD AND DATE OF APPROVAL:
SCOPE OF APPROVAL:

IF NO, PLEASE STATE IF THE ORGANISATION HAS:
    A QUALITY MANUAL?   [YES | NO]
    DOCUMENTED PROCEDURES FOR:
        INSPECTION OF PURCHASED MATERIAL?   [YES | NO]
        PROCESS CONTROLS/INSPECTIONS?   [YES | NO]
        INSPECTION OF FINISHED PRODUCT?   [YES | NO]
        CALIBRATION OF INSPECTION/TEST EQUIPMENT?   [YES | NO]

    ARE FORMAL RECORDS KEPT TO SUPPORT
    THESE PROCEDURES?   [YES | NO]

    ARE YOU WILLING FOR YOUR SYSTEMS AND PROCEDURES
    TO BE EVALUATED BY EXTERNAL ASSESSORS?   [YES | NO]

SIGNED: NAME: POSITION: DATE:

Ref: SAQ-01, Issue 1, August 1993

ATMOSTAT CONTROLS LTD
JOB DESCRIPTION

SERVICE MANAGER
Department: Service department
Responsible to: Technical director

DUTIES

1 To ensure that:
   • installations of all the company's products are planned and carried out;
   • planned maintenance programmes for customers' equipment are devised and implemented;
   • failures and breakdowns of customers' equipment are promptly and effectively repaired;
   in accordance with the company standards and the requirements of the customers.

2 To provide technical advice and expertise to existing and prospective customers, and other company departments.

3 To ensure that the company quality policy and procedures are implemented and developed within the department.

4 To ensure that departmental training plans are devised and implemented.

5 To provide leadership and management of the departmental staff.

6 To assist in the production of the annual budget for the department and manage the department's resources within that budget.

7 To provide such historical and statistical data as may be required by the directors concerning the activities of the department.

8 To contribute to the effectiveness of the company management team as a whole, and undertake additional duties as may be considered necessary or appropriate from time to time.

STANDARDS OF PERFORMANCE

Satisfactory customer service.
Operation of the department to within budget.
Satisfactory performance of department staff.
Satisfactory results from internal and external audits.

RESOURCES

Budget, staffing and equipment levels as agreed with technical director.

AUTHORITY

To define targets and standards of performance for the department subject to the approval of the technical director.
Limit of spending without Board approval: £10,000.
Management of staff in accordance with company personnel policies.

Approved, M.D._____date_____Accepted, S.M._____date_____

ATMOSTAT CONTROLS LTD
MINUTES OF QUARTERLY MANAGEMENT QUALITY
REVIEW MEETING, 10 JANUARY 1995, HEAD OFFICE

Present: Alex Smart, managing director
                  Peter Prolific, production director
                  David Wizard, technical director
                  Jim Ikan, production manager
                  Steve Sparkle, design manager
                  Alan Tinker, service manager
                  John Steadfast, quality manager (Chair)

Apologies: George Swindel, commercial director

Initials in **bold type** indicate those responsible for action.

1 J.S. reported that all systems were working very well, with the exception that some internal audits were behind schedule due to pressure of work on auditors. Agreed to train more supervisory staff as auditors, each department manager to nominate one supervisor to go on external course scheduled in February.

D.W., J.I., S.S., A.T.

2 J.S. reported that too much raw material was bypassing the receiving inspections because of hold-ups in receiving inspection. Agreed that J.I. and J.S. investigate the financial implications of either increasing buffer stocks or employing an extra receiving inspector; report back to February management meeting.

J.I., J.S.

3 J.S. reported that supplier problems continued to reduce, with average reject rates down to 1.15 per cent. Acme Ltd's returns still caused some concern though at 4 per cent D.W. and G.S. to look for alternative supplier.

D.W., G.S.

4 No external quality audits had taken place since last meeting.

5 Training: following interviews, four candidates have been selected for short-listing for the post of training manager. It is expected that the post will be filled by the end of February.

A.S.

6 In the absence of the commercial director, J.S. gave the three-monthly summary of customer complaints. Concern was expressed about the increasing rate of thermostat failures. Agreed to hold discussions with suppliers about improving their specification, and in the mean time, to give 100 per cent inspection to all thermostats in receiving inspection.

A.S., J.S.

cont.

ATMOSTAT CONTROLS LTD

MINUTES OF QUARTERLY MANAGEMENT QUALITY REVIEW MEETING, 10 January 1995, Page 2 (cont.)

7 Major corrective actions during the last quarter included:

1 Reducing the speed of printed circuits through the flow-soldering machine; this has resulted in a reduction of non-conformities due to dry joints of 32 per cent.

2 Redesign of the packaging of the Mk III controller. This has reduced the incidence of breakage of the indicator lamp in transit to nil.

3 Reprogramming the control unit of the Enviro-Master. This, however, has not reduced the incidence of trip-out, and further work is required by the design department.

P.P.

8 The quality manager closed the meeting with a reminder that the pre-assessment visit from the approval body is due on 3 February. Agreed that all managers and supervisors ensure that all their systems and records are up-to-date in preparation.

ALL

Minutes recorded by J. D. Smith, secretary to directors.

ATMOSTAT CONTROLS LTD
INTERNAL AUDIT REPORT

Date of audit:	9 December 1994	No: RI/94/02

Scope of audit: Receiving Inspection procedures and documentation.

Purpose of audit: To establish conformance of the audited department to the requirements of the company's quality system and those of BS EN ISO 9001, 1994.

To establish the adequacy of the quality systems for the effective control of incoming raw materials.

Location of audit: Receiving inspection area and office.

References: BS EN ISO 9001, 1994, clause 4.10,
QM-01, Issue 1, Quality Manual,
PROC-05, Issue 1, Inspection and Testing

Auditor: John Smith

Distribution: Quality manager,
Receiving inspection supervisor.

1. THE AUDIT

1.1 The audit was previously scheduled for Tuesday 7 December, but was postponed until the 9th at the request of the receiving inspection supervisor due to staff sickness on the 7th.

1.2 The auditor was accompanied throughout the audit by the receiving inspection supervisor, Mary Jones. She and her staff of inspectors and testers were at all times helpful and co-operative.

1.3 Ref. PROC-05, 2.1 and 2.10. Records of material being passed directly to production for processing without inspection were being kept in a notebook; there is no official document for this purpose, although the records were comprehensive and complete.

At least 5 per cent of all purchased material bypassed receiving inspection during November 1994. Mary Jones stated that this was because she was continually short staffed and production was always requiring material urgently.

1.4 ITP-1045, ITP-1046 and ITP-1047, Inspection/Test Procedures in the department's master folder were found to be Issue 1, when the current issue 2 was circulated on 30 November 1994. On pointing this out Miss Jones stated that she had received the updated procedures, but had yet to replace them in the master folder. The situation was corrected immediately.

ATMOSTAT CONTROLS LTD
INTERNAL AUDIT REPORT

AUDIT REPORT RI/94/02 (cont.)

1.5 The documentation of the department was completed exceptionally well, in particular the RIREP-01, Receiving Inspection Report, being clear and legible and immediately to hand for any date.

1.6 Ref. QM-01 section 15, Product Identification and Traceability. Some un-identifiable components had been left in a tray on an unoccupied bench. These had apparently been there for some weeks; no one was able to relate them to any order or delivery, but one inspector stated that he thought they had been left by a visiting sales representative. They were immediately classified as non-conforming product.

1.7 Ref. PROC-05, 2.6. A box of heating elements labelled as non-conforming product was found among similar items that had passed inspection. No corresponding Non-conformity Report was found. On enquiry, it was dis-covered that an inspector was in the process of raising the non-conformity prior to going to lunch, but had omitted to complete the process on his return. He was instructed to complete the paperwork immediately and remove the heating elements to the non-conforming product area.

1.8 Ref. QM-01, section 18. All measuring and test equipment was found to be within its calibration period and labelled accordingly. However, an uncalibrated spring balance was found on a shelf. This was removed to a desk drawer.

1.9 Apart from the deficiencies above, the quality systems were found to be implemented and maintained fully in the department. All staff when ques-tioned were aware of their duties and responsibilities with regard to the quality system, and were able to demonstrate their understanding.

The inspection area and office were generally tidy and clean, and, with the exception of the above items, everything was in the correct place.

2. CONCLUSIONS

2.1 In general the systems in the department were managed very well, with a small number of deficiencies. Miss Jones was anxious about these and immediately addressed those that she could.

It is clear that the department was understaffed, causing delays in the inspection and testing, and the consequent use of uninspected/untested material.

3. RECOMMENDATIONS

3.1 An official form is needed to record the passing of uninspected/untested

ATMOSTAT CONTROLS LTD
INTERNAL AUDIT REPORT

AUDIT REPORT RI/94/02 (cont.)

materials to production. Mary Jones is to propose a format and discuss with the quality manager by 13 December 1994.

3.2 The issue of short-staffing/overwork in the department needs to be addressed to make the department more efficient. By receipt of a copy of this report the quality manager is requested to take some urgent action.

3.3 Attention must be given to more careful housekeeping, especially relating to:

- updating documentation promptly;
- strict use of non-conforming product procedures;
- unidentified material in the area;
- uncalibrated equipment.

Miss Jones promised an immediate improvement.

3.4 Because of the excellent way records have been kept in the department, it is suggested that Mary Jones become involved in training of documentary procedures. She has expressed an interest in doing this although she feels her involvement cannot take place while the department is so overloaded. She will discuss this with the quality manager at their next scheduled meeting on 13 December.

3.5 The uncalibrated spring balance must be permanently removed from the department, or clearly marked 'not for use' at the earliest possible time.

4. FUTURE ACTION

4.1 Based on the findings of this audit, no further follow-up is considered necessary until the next scheduled audit in June 1995.

Signed:_____Auditor, Date: 9 December 1994

SECTION D

APPENDICES

STANDARDS: BS EN ISO 9000 SERIES

BS EN ISO 9001, 1994: Specification for design/development, production, installation and servicing.

BS EN ISO 9002, 1994: Specification for production, installation and servicing.

BS EN ISO 9003, 1994: Specification for final inspection and test.

OTHER REFERENCE MATERIAL

BS 5750, part 4, 1995: Guide to the use of BS EN ISO 9000.

BS 5750, part 8, 1991: Guide to quality management and quality system elements for services. (Currently in the course of revision; an amendment dated December 1993 is avilable in the meantime.)

BSI Guide to the 1994 Revision of BS 5750/ISO 9000: Ref. E313, Issue 1.

The above are published by:

British Standards Institution,
2 Park Street,
London W1A 2BS
Tel: 0171 629 9000

and are available through HMSO outlets.

SOURCES OF FURTHER INFORMATION ABOUT QUALITY INITIATIVES AND FUNDING

Department of Trade and Industry 0171 627 7800 (enquire for regional numbers)

Scottish Development Agency 0131 346 9170

Welsh Development Agency 01443 841200

The 85 Training and Enterprise Councils offer various schemes to help local organisations achieve BS EN ISO 9000 accreditation, for example, with seminars, workshops, courses and subsidised consultancy. Look in your local telephone directory for the TEC that serves your area.

Universities and colleges frequently offer training, joint workshops and other assistance, including student out-placements, to help with quality system implementation.

Your local Chamber of Commerce will be a good scource of information about any activity regarding quality initiatives and schemes in the area.

LIST OF APPROVAL BODIES (ACCREDITED INDEPENDENT THIRD PARTY CERTIFICATION BODIES)

ABS Quality Evaluations Ltd
ABS House, 1 Frying Pan Alley, London E1 7HS
Tel: 0171 377 2622

Associated Offices Quality Certification Ltd
Longridge House, Longridge Place, Manchester M60 4DT
Tel: 0161 833 2295

ASTA Certification Services
ASTA House, Chestnut Field, Rugby, Warwickshire CV21 3TL
Tel: 01788 578435

BMT Quality Assessors Ltd
Scottish Metropolitan Alpha Centre, Stirling University Innovation Park, Stirling FK9 4NF
Tel: 01786 450891

British Approvals Service for Cables (BASEC)
Silbury Court, 360 Silbury Boulevard, Milton Keynes MK9 2AF
Tel: 01908 691121

BSI Quality Assurance (BSIQA)
PO Box 375, Milton Keynes MK14 6LL
Tel: 01908 220908

Bureau Veritas Quality International Ltd (BVQI)
70 Borough High Street, London SE1 1XF
Tel: 0171 378 8113

Central Certification Service (CCS)
Ambron House, Eastfield Road, Wellingborough, Northants NN8 1QX
Tel: 01933 441796

Ceramic Industry Certification Scheme Ltd (CICS)
Queens Road, Penkull, Stoke-on-Trent ST4 7LQ
Tel: 01782 411008

Construction Quality Assurance (CQA)
Barnby House, Barnby Gate, Newark, Notts NG24 1PZ
Tel: 01636 708700

Det Norske Veritas Quality Assurance Ltd (DNVQA)
Palace House, 3 Cathedral Street, London SE1 9DE
Tel: 0171 357 6080

Electrical Equipment Certification Service
Health & Safety Executive, Harpur Hill, Buxton, Derbyshire SK17 9JN
Tel: 01298 28000

Electricity Association Quality Assurance Ltd (EAQA)
30 Millbank, London SW1P 4RD
Tel: 0171 344 5947

Engineering Inspection Authorities Board (EIAB)
The Institution of Mechanical Engineers, 1 Birdcage Walk,
London SW1H 9JJ
Tel: 0171 973 1271

Global Certification Ltd
The Old School, Leicester Road, Groby, Leicestershire LE6 0DQ
Tel: 0116 287 7700

INSPEC Certification Ltd
The Buckland Wharf, Aylesbury, Bucks HP22 5LQ
Tel: 01296 631350

Inspectorate of the Security Industry
Security House, Barbourne Road, Worcester WR1 1RS
Tel: 01905 617499

ISO Quality Assured Register (ISOQAR)
Suite 7, City Park Business Village, Cornbrook, Manchester M16 9HQ
Tel: 0161 877 6914

Lloyds Register Quality Assurance Ltd (LRQA)
Hiramford, Middlemarch Office Village, Siskin Drive, Coventry CV3 4FJ
Tel: 01203 639566

Marketing Quality Assurance Ltd
Operations Directorate, Midsummer House, 435 Midsummer Boulevard,
Central Milton Keynes MK3 3BN
Tel: 01908 231565

NAFEMS QA Ltd,
NEL Technology Park, East Kilbride, Glasgow G75 0QU
Tel: 0135 5272027

National Approval Council for Security Systems (NACOSS)
Queensgate House, 14 Cookham Road, Maidenhead, Berks SL6 8AJ
Tel: 01628 37512

National Quality Assurance Ltd
26 Stuart Street, Luton LU1 2SW
Tel: 01582 488448

Offer (EMMS) Electricity Meter Measurements Service
Hagley House, Hagley Road, Edgbaston, Birmingham B16 8QG
Tel: 0121 456 2100

PECS Professional Environmental & Caring Services (QA) Ltd
Resource House, 144 High Street, Rayleigh, Essex SS6 7BU
Tel: 01268 770135

Personnel Certification in Non-Destructive Testing
1 Spencer Parade, Northampton NN1 5AA
Tel: 01604 30124

Premier Assessments Ltd
The Derwent Business Centre, Unit 40, Clarke Street, Derby DE1 2BU
Tel: 01332 202556

Quality Certification Ltd
Rowland House, 15 Chelsea Field Estate, Western Road,
London SW19 2QA
Tel: 0181 646 8383

RAC Quality Assurance Ltd
RAC House, Bartlett Street, South Croydon, Surrey CR2 6XW
Tel: 0181 686 0088

SIRA Certification Service
Saighton Lane, Saighton, Chester CH3 6EG
Tel: 01244 336885

Steel Construction Quality Assurance Scheme Ltd (SCQAS)
4 Whitehall Court, Westminster, London SW1A 2ES
Tel: 0171 839 8566

The Loss Prevention Certification Board Ltd (LPCB)
Melrose Avenue, Borehamwood, Hertfordshire WD6 2BJ
Tel: 0181 207 2345

The Quality Scheme for Ready Mixed Concrete (QSRMC)
3 High Street, Hampton, Middlesex TW12 2SQ
Tel: 0181 941 0273

TRADA Quality Assurance Services Ltd
Stocking Lane, Hughenden Valley, High Wycombe, Bucks HP14 4NR
Tel: 01240 245484

TWI (Certification Scheme for Welding and Inspection Personnel)
Abingdon Hall, Abingdon, Cambridge CB1 6AL
Tel: 01223 891162

UK Certification Authority for Reinforcing Steels (CARES)
Oak House, Tubs Hill, Sevenoaks, Kent TN13 1BL
Tel: 01732 450000

Vehicle Certification Agency
1 The Eastgate Office Centre, Eastgate House, Bristol BS5 6XX
Tel: 0117 951 5151

Water Industry Certification Scheme (WICS)
Frankland Road, Blagrove, Swindon SN5 8YF
Tel: 01793 410005

WIMLAS Ltd
Beaconsfield Road, Hayes, Middlesex UB4 0LS
Tel: 0181 573 7744

Yardsley Quality Assured Firms Ltd (YQAF)
Trowers Way, Redhill, Surrey RH1 2JN
Tel: 01737 768445

RECOGNISED SECOND PARTY ASSESSMENT BODIES

British Gas Plc
Hinckley Operational Centre, QS & QA Vendor Appraisals, Brick Kiln Street, Hinckley, Leicestershire LE10 0NA
Tel: 01455 251111

British Rail Quality Assurance Services
Derwent House, Railway Technical Centre, London Road,
Derby DE24 8UP
Tel: 01332 262763

National Grid Company Plc
Burymead House, Portsmouth Road, Guildford, Surrey GU2 5BN
Tel: 01483 507197

The above lists were compiled in February 1995. For further information, contact:

The National Accreditation Council for Certification Bodies
Audley House, 13 Palace Street, London SW1E 5HS
Tel: 0171 233 7111

INDEX

Dear Pitman Publishing Customer

IMPORTANT – Read This Now!

We are delighted to announce a special free service for all of our customers.

Simply complete this form and return it to the address overleaf to receive:

A Free Customer Newsletter

B Free Information Service

C Exclusive Customer Offers – which have included free software, videos and relevant products

D Opportunity to take part in product development sessions

E The chance for you to write about your own business experience and become one of our respected authors

Fill this in now and return it to us (no stamp needed in the UK) to join our customer information service.

Name: _____ Position: _____

Company/Organisation: _____

Address (including postcode): _____

Country: _____

Telephone: _____ Fax: _____

Nature of business: _____

Title of book purchased: _____

Comments: _____

- | **Fold Here Then Staple** | -

We would be very grateful if you could answer these questions to help us with market research.

1 Where/How did you hear of this book?

☐ in a bookshop

☐ in a magazine/newspaper (please state which):

☐ information through the post

☐ recommendation from a colleague

☐ other (please state which):

2 Which newspaper(s)/magazine(s) do you read regularly?:

3 When buying a business book which factors influence you most?
(Please rank in order)

☐ recommendation from a colleague

☐ price

☐ content

☐ recommendation in a bookshop

☐ author

☐ publisher

☐ title

☐ other(s):

4 Is this book a

☐ personal purchase?

☐ company purchase?

5 Would you be prepared to spend a few minutes talking to our customer services staff to help with product development? YES/NO